MW01706596

She Laughed
All the Way to the Bank

She Laughed All the Way to the Bank

Financial Empowerment for Canadian Women

Cindy Skrukwa

RAINCOAST BOOKS
Vancouver

First published in 2000 by Raincoast Books,
8680 Cambie Street, Vancouver, B.C.
V6P 6M9
(604) 323-7100
www.raincoast.com

1 2 3 4 5 6 7 8 9 10

CANADIAN CATALOGUING IN PUBLICATION DATA

Skrukwa, Cindy
She laughed all the way to the bank

Includes bibliographical references,
ISBN 1-55192-282-7

1. Women-Canada-Finance, Personal, I. Title.
HG179.S49 1999 332.024'042 C99-910973-1

Editing by Joanne Richardson
Inside Design by Hermani & Sorrentino Design
Cover Illustration & Design by Michela Sorrentino
Printed in Canada

The Canada Council for the Arts since 1957 | Le Conseil des Arts du Canada depuis 1957

Raincoast Books gratefully acknowledges the support of the Government of Canada, through the Book Publishing Industry Development Program, the Canada Council and the Department of Canadian Heritage. We also acknowledge the assistance of the Province of British Columbia, through the British Columbia Arts Council.

This book is dedicated to the spirit of my grandmother,
Dr. Edith Maria Gruber – a woman who taught me, by example,
that every woman has the right and the power
to shape her own journey through life.

Contents

Making the Most of the Financial Freedom You've Earned

Introduction

...and he said: You pretty full of yourself ain't chu so she replied: Show me someone not full of herself and I'll show you a hungry person.

Nikki Giovanni

During the summer of 1996 I took a wonderful vacation that, unbeknownst to me, would give birth to the idea of writing this book. It seemed innocent enough, a week in Tofino with my sister, visiting two friends – all of us single women near the 30-year mark in our lives.

The trip was great. The locals we met through our friends were incredibly hospitable. We ate fabulous meals of fresh seafood straight from the dock and the sun shone every day. The highlight of the trip was our visit to a private nature reserve. The island was stunning. Inhabited only by the owner and a grounds-keeping couple, it was a paradise of beautiful mossy forest, filled with rambling paths and surrounded by blonde, sandy beach. Our afternoon hike ended up being one of those special occasions in life when I think to myself, "This is a truly outstanding moment."

As amazing as the island was, one thing made the experience even more meaningful for me. The island belonged to a woman. A woman – not a man, not a couple – one independent woman controlled the island.

At the time, I was working as a marketing manager for a multinational corporation in Toronto and was constantly bombarded with information about successful men: men who owned things, men who did deals, men of political importance. At my firm and in virtually every major global corporation, senior management positions and the power that goes with them were concentrated in the hands of men. And even though my employer was making attempts to prepare more women for senior roles, these were only attainable if you played by male rules and were willing to sacrifice most other parts of your life. Deep down I knew it was unfair and unbalanced, and, frankly, I was tired of it.

One night, my friends and I drank wine and talked. By the end of the evening our conversation had turned to money and personal finances. Soon I was reviewing Lisa's company savings plan and advising her on which investments I thought were best for her. Then we talked about Andrea's condominium and how she had managed to purchase it with her sister. Soon it became apparent that, of the entire group, including a forester, a teacher, a medical doctor and myself, only I, with six years of university business education, really understood the basics of personal financial management. My three companions began urging me to write down what I was telling them. "It all seemed pretty straightforward when you explained it," they said. "It's just pouring out of you, and you've always been the one who never seemed to lack money. Even when we were all students, paying our own way through school, you always had savings. Share what you know with other women!"

Upon my return from Tofino I went back to work and filed the book idea away under the category of "maybe some day." At the same time, my satisfaction with my work life was eroding. In the three and a half years I'd been with my employer, the week in Tofino was one of the longest vacations I had taken. Work was constantly on my mind; I even dreamed about it. I felt disillusioned with the male dominance, both physically and culturally, in the management ranks at my firm and throughout industry. One particularly abrasive male co-worker was waging a personal campaign to undermine my confidence.

I made a decision that many of my colleagues thought was crazy: I turned down a large promotion. After months of soul-searching, I had concluded that choosing my dream career path would severely hamper the probability of being able to live my dream life. I wanted a more holistic life, even if that meant shifting my career aspirations to make room for the rest of me. I quit and moved back to my native Alberta to begin a new chapter of my journey.

In Alberta, I moved to a lower-profile, lower-stress position, but the transition was tough. Up until that point, I'd spent my entire life achieving. I had graduated from my MBA program as the top student in my class. I had worked on Fifth Avenue in New York City. I had been trained to compete and win. I missed the ego strokes and excitement of my high-flying career.

Realizing I still wasn't happy, nine months after I arrived in Alberta I quit my job to focus on writing this book. I also began consulting in order to generate some extra income. I now balance consulting, writing, personal reflection and lots of social activity. I'm well on my way to building the life I truly want rather than pursuing the path that seemed to represent "what I was supposed to do."

I never would have summoned the courage or the means to walk away from employment and contemplate the possibility of a year off without pay if I hadn't been saving and investing since I started earning money at age 14. I believe I have a simple philosophy about money and that it has served me well. My goal is to share it with you.

I'm also excited about revealing the inspiring insights and attitudes I've discovered through interviews with many intriguing and generous Canadian women. From these women I learned that attitude is the most important factor in determining your financial success or failure. As a result, a significant portion of this book is dedicated to helping you uncover your hidden beliefs about money and to tracing their origins. By removing personal mental blocks to prosperity, you will be able to develop a personal financial vision and goals as well as enhancing the way you interact with money.

Compare making a financial plan to trying to lose weight. You need to understand why you overeat, in addition to knowing what is healthy to eat, before you can succeed in long-term weight control. Once you've cleared the internal blocks it is much easier to set realistic weight loss goals and to stick to good eating habits. Likewise, financially, you need to understand why you interact with money the way you do, plus the basic techniques of good money management, before you can consistently execute a sensible personal financial plan. This book is designed to help you do this.

She Laughed All the Way to the Bank covers the basics of investing and shares real-life stories concerning how various women's decisions have affected their financial health. Many of these women have achieved a great deal financially and are happy to explain how they have succeeded. I hope this inspires you to realize your own strength and empowers you to move ahead financially. I hope it leaves you feeling more confident about making the decisions that will help you take better care of yourself, no matter what your marital status or stage of life. I hope it leaves you laughing all the way to the bank.

Acknowledgements

If I learned one lesson while writing this book, it is that if you really want to achieve something, the ways and means by which to achieve it will appear and people all around you will do what they can to help you reach your goal.

I am extremely grateful to the many generous individuals who contributed to this project:

To the forthright women who honestly shared their stories for no other reason than to help others;

To my many informal editors, particularly my sister Monica, for reading and enthusiastically commenting on the many iterations of this book;

To the many supportive friends, colleagues, librarians, financial professionals and publishing professionals who helped and encouraged me throughout;

And to my Higher Power.

Thank you all. I couldn't have done it alone.

Disclaimer

Some names and non-essential details have been altered to protect the privacy of individuals referred to in this book. Also, at times, quoted material has been paraphrased to enhance readability while maintaining the underlying content.

This book is designed to provide accurate and valid information on the subject matter. It has been carefully researched and verified for accuracy; however, due to the complexity and changing nature of the subject matter, neither the author nor the publisher can be held responsible for errors or omissions, or for the consequences of any action resulting from the information in this book. Examples discussed are intended as general guidelines only.

This book is sold with the understanding that neither the author nor the publisher is engaged in rendering legal and accounting advice or opinions. If such advice or opinions are required, then the reader is urged to seek the services of a competent and experienced professional.

Every reasonable effort has been made to obtain permission for all articles and data used in this edition. If errors or omissions have occurred, they will be corrected in future editions provided written notification has been received by the publisher.

The quote from Sister Mary Madeleva at the start of Chapter 6 is used with permission of the Congregation of the Sisters of the Holy Cross.

The pronoun "she" has been used throughout for simplicity's sake to refer to individuals who could be either male or female.

1

The Big Picture

Money is like a sixth sense without which you cannot make a complete use of the other five.

W. Somerset Maugham

Success comes in many forms in life; material wealth is only one and, generally, not the most important one. Without your health, love and a sense of purpose, all of the money in the world will not make you happy. Nevertheless, there is no denying that a lack of money has made many people miserable.

Financial security can smooth the path, provide increased options in the pursuit of non-monetary goals and strengthen your confidence and peace of mind. Paying attention to your money – controlling it rather than letting it control you – feels good and can actually be fun. When you are on top of your financial situation you get a kick out of reviewing your finances and finding that you have $5,000 more than you did last time around. You like thinking about all of the ways you could spend or, more likely, invest that money. It makes you feel good – proud of what you are achieving and secure that every additional dollar contributes to your ability to choose what you do and do not want to do with your life. You feel confident that you have options. You don't have to stay at jobs you don't enjoy, you don't have to stay in relationships you don't enjoy, you don't have to do anything you don't want to do for lack of money. You can decide to embark on riskier career paths, and you can pursue intriguing adventures. You have choices.

The fact is, money matters in our society. Its possession provides power and choice for many people. Yet, you may not be experiencing all of the positive benefits of financial abundance in your life; you may still be uncomfortable and unclear about how to make the most of your money. This book is designed to help you understand why you may not be experiencing all of the financial prosperity available to you and how you can improve your financial situation, regardless of your current income or level of wealth.

None of us is perfect at managing our money, but most of us could be enjoying a lot more prosperity than we are currently. In my experience, the most common reasons we give ourselves for not making the most of our money include:[1]

- I don't know where to start.
- I don't know what to do.
- It takes too much time.
- I associate financial prosperity with negative traits such as greed.
- I'm scared that paying attention to my own financial security will threaten my partner.

None of these reasons needs to stop you from taking action. All of these fears and challenges are addressed in *She Laughed All the Way to the Bank*. You will see that there are easy ways to manage your money – ways that don't take more than an hour or two a month. You'll learn new ways to increase your income and how to improve your financial situation. Most important, negative conscious and unconscious beliefs about money, which may be slowing you down, will be examined and challenged because, as you change your mind, you change your actions and you change your life. Last, we'll discuss the importance, and significant benefits, of staying involved with your finances throughout your life as well as how to ensure that your prosperity is preserved, regardless of your romantic status.

You've Already Come a Long Way!

The stage is set. Not only do you have the information you need in the form of this book, but, historically, you are living in the right time to be able, as a woman, to make the most of your finances. This hasn't always been the case.

Not long ago, women's lack of access to material possessions and title severely limited their options in life. Little more than 100 years ago married Canadian women were not considered to be legally separate from their husbands. This meant that they could not independently enter into contracts and that their husbands had complete ownership of all family property.[2]

Even 20 years ago, Canadian women still faced many overt hurdles on the road to financial prosperity. One woman I interviewed told me that when she was divorced during the 1970s the banks refused to give her a mortgage even though she had been employed for over 10 years in a well-paying sales position. She recalls the bank manager unabashedly telling her, "We don't give mortgages to divorced women."

Another story, this one with a happy ending, came from Trisha, a bank vice-president. I asked her how she decided to go into banking. "The decision to join the bank was made for me," she replied. "I was happily employed as a clerk for the Hudson's Bay Company, in Men's Wear. A steady stream of young and eligible men came in to shop. I met my first husband that way. Once we were married, he would come in and pick me up on Friday nights. In the end, the store offered him a job as a manager. It was company policy that husband and wife couldn't both work there at the same time, so they hired him and told me to find another job."

Trisha found a new job as the mail girl at the local bank. Luckily for her, the bank was a progressive organization, and, 25 years later, she is a regional vice-president. As she says, "It was the best thing that ever happened."

Nowadays I can't imagine a woman being pushed out of an organization to make room for her husband; instead, women are increasingly active in the workforce and in providing for their families. Women are starting their own businesses in record numbers, and almost half of RRSP contributors are female.

We are making great strides in many areas that directly affect our financial well-being and the power that goes along with having financial clout. Women now make up over half of our country's law and medical students and 45 percent of corporate middle management.[3] From 1980 to 1995, the average Canadian woman's income rose by 15 percent, whereas the average male's income actually declined by over seven percent after adjusting for inflation.[4] During the same period, the number of Canadian woman making over $50,000 per year increased by 150 percent.[5]

Nevertheless, we are still under-represented with regard to the accumulation of wealth. Although three out of eight Canadian adults own stock, two-thirds of these owners are men.[6] At the same time, 56 percent of elderly Canadian women are living alone and in poverty.[7] Facing an average of 15 years of retirement, and most likely at least a decade of that without a mate, it is a good thing that you are taking responsibility for your financial prosperity now. Money provides security, and security is definitely something that you want in your old age, if not sooner.

So how do we create financial security for ourselves? The answer is in the "Prosperity Equation."

The Prosperity Equation

The prosperity equation sums up all of the levers you can adjust to maximize money and its benefits in your life. Each element is important; each builds on the others.

Cultivate positive money attitudes	$
+ Waste less	$ $
+ Earn more	$ $ $
+ Invest wisely	$ $ $ $
+ Protect what you have	$ $ $ $ $
Achieve your financial goals	$ $ $ $ $ $
Achieve your life goals	♥♥♥♥♥♥♥

Ultimately, the more mastery you have over this equation, the more likely you are to achieve your heart's desire – your deepest life goals. Whether your dream is to be a mother, to climb the Himalayas, to preserve the environment, to pursue spiritual enlightenment or all of the above, money can help you get there. I'm not saying it will get you there – that depends on your free will and choice – but it can pave the road.

"How can money help me become a mother?" you ask. Well, your savings might provide you with the option of spending more time in your role as mother once you have children rather than focusing on earning income to pay the bills. If you are single, your money could provide you with the financial security to consider becoming a mother on your own. Or maybe your money could support your dream of starting an after-school art program, where you could mother underprivileged children. Really, the number of paths leading to your life ambitions, which can be paved with money, is limited only by your imagination.

In the following chapters, we explore each essential ingredient of the prosperity equation. I will guide you in figuring out what you really believe about money and where those beliefs came from. You'll see that it is not what you earn, but what you believe about money that has the biggest impact on your financial prosperity. You'll learn to cultivate positive internal prosperity messages. Next, we'll explore the habits of women who save painlessly and who actually enjoy making decisions about what not to buy as much as they enjoy making decisions about what to buy. The section on increasing your income will address the topics of career selection, how to increase your income within a given job, how to increase your overall employment market value and the option of self-employment. The investing chapters contain everything you need to know about investing your money wisely, and you may be surprised at how simple it really is, once the industry jargon is removed. Last, we will discuss how to protect your wealth throughout your life so that you can maximize its contribution to you and your loved ones.

The Bottom Line

This is not so much a book about getting rich as it is a book about enhancing your financial strength. It is about learning more about generating financial prosperity in your life and applying these lessons so that you can use your financial strength to buy yourself freedom, choice and expanded options in the pursuit of your life goals.

I hope you enjoy the journey and learn from the experiences of the women who candidly share their stories. Take away what you like – an idea, a tip, a new awareness or more – and apply it in your life. And feel a little prouder and more confident because women everywhere are taking control of their fortunes – both financial and otherwise – and you can too.

2

How Do You Define Success?

The secret of success is constancy of purpose.

BENJAMIN DISRAELI

Although this book covers all of the basics of saving and investing, its central theme is that money should play a supporting role in your life, not a starring role. Taking ownership of your own financial situation – being informed about money and making educated financial decisions – makes you more powerful and confident, not just in financial matters, but in general. This is because, like all the parts of the universe, all the parts of your life – your universe – are intertwined. Shifts in one area invariably affect other areas, so your relationship with money is important not just because it can lead to material wealth, but also because it can help you succeed in other areas of your life.

Have you ever noticed that when you take care of problems in one area of your life other areas often seem to improve at the same time? Maybe when you start working on your health, things seem to improve at work, or when you sort out grievances with your co-workers, your relationship with your mother improves as well? Partially, this is because you naturally transfer new skills that you learn in one part of your life to other parts. However, it is also because your new and improved attitudes expand beyond the part of your life in which you are succeeding. There are no hard and fast boundaries separating your love life from your financial life, your spiritual life or any other part of your life. Positive changes in one area of your life naturally spill over into other areas because all aspects of your life take up residence inside your mind and spirit. Happiness in one corner of your brain is bound to shine on other regions and give the whole landscape a lift. Money floats through it all, sometimes invisibly, sometimes glaringly obviously. Keeping your financial matters in good condition pays off, not just at the bank, but also in your confidence level, your energy level and your ability to achieve non-monetary goals. So what are you waiting for?

Many people attach a lot of guilt to the idea of having money. We have all heard the biblical quote about it being harder for a rich man to pass through the gates of heaven than for a camel to pass through the eye of a needle. Some people assume that managing your money well implies that you are materialistic and that materialism equals "bad." Are ideas like these holding you back?

You can choose to look at it a lot differently. You can view money as a tool – an enabler that increases your freedom to choose your path in life. Money allows you to take advantage of opportunities. With money, you can choose to do things that will have a positive impact on the people in your life and the world around you. Financial prosperity can be a very positive force in your life, if you so choose.

I chose to write this book and to share what I've learned. I believe this book will have a positive influence on many women. Without having had money in the bank, which allowed me to step away from full-time corporate life, I would not have made this choice.

The Paradox

Herein lies the paradox: the less attention you pay to your finances now, the more likely you are to be plagued by time-consuming financial difficulties later. The less attention you pay to managing your money proactively, the more time and energy money matters are likely to consume in your life. You can't avoid money. Money is a powerful force in your life whether you want it to be or not. There is no escaping it. By investing some time and effort in understanding how to use money effectively to support your life goals, and by developing good money management habits, you are more likely to end up having far fewer money worries. Instead of being a source of aggravation and grief, your money can become exactly what it should be – a means towards accomplishing your life's mission.

In this book you will meet Sandra, a clinical psychologist in her fifties with a self-made $2,000,000 investment portfolio. Sandra has choices. She chooses to keep practising as a therapist because she wants to, and she continues to reinvest her money rather than retire and live off of it because she loves the thrill of investing. You'll meet Ellen, who, in her mid-thirties, looks back at all of the hard work and scrimping she and her husband did to pay off their 3,000-square-foot home and is thrilled that she can now choose to be a stay-at-home mom with her young sons. They and plenty of other women will tell you how they took control of their money and put it to work for them rather than vice versa.

Sandra and Ellen decided early on that the peace of mind they got from having savings to fall back on was more important to them than the instant gratification of impulse purchases. By picking a few "spending priorities" that they were not willing to give up, and by saying "No" to other non-necessities, they ended up having far more opportunity to enjoy the things that were really important to them.

Where Are You Headed?

In 1967, stockbroker Muriel Siebert became the first woman to own a seat on the New York Stock Exchange; she was also the first woman to serve as superintendent of banks for the State of New York. Women have been advancing and excelling in the world of finance ever since. By determining your priorities and following a few simple steps, you too can excel in your own personal world of finance.

What is your vision of success for yourself? Is it being a good parent? Is it travelling the world? Is it owning your own company? Looking beyond money to the big picture, what is it that you really want to achieve in this lifetime? Not just financially, but also in the realms of relationships, career, spirituality and health. If you were independently wealthy, what is it that you would do with your time? Picture what you would do, for in that image you will see the essential ingredients of your life's mission, and it is with this image that you should start your financial planning.

Think back over the experiences you've had, the places you've lived and the lessons you've learned. When were you most fulfilled? Does this give you further insight into your life's mission?

Marva, a single, 28-year-old, part-time university student and waitress, defines her life goals as:

1. To have my own family and maintain a close circle of friends
2. To own my own retail business
3. To have a balanced lifestyle with time for spiritual growth and physical exercise
4. To own my own home and have enough retirement income to maintain a reasonable lifestyle and travel occasionally
5. To explore and experience different cultures

As we work through the prosperity equation we will revisit Marva's goals and help her to translate them into specific financial actions that she can begin to put in place now. You will have the opportunity to clarify your life goals in the "Making It Happen" exercise at the end of this chapter. Please take the time to really think about this. To succeed financially you first need to clarify your non-monetary goals. Money is merely an enabler, and once you know what you want your money to help you achieve in the grander scheme of things, you'll be much more motivated to build the financial footing that can help you get from here to there.

Surfing for Opportunity

Not only does being clear about your vision for the future increase your motivation to build the financial underpinnings of that vision, it also allows you to effectively take advantage of opportunities that appear in your path. I call this "surfing for opportunities." What I mean by this is that if you are clear on where you want to end up, you are much more likely to see opportunities that will take you in the general direction of your long-term goals, and you will be much more likely to act promptly on them.

For instance, imagine that you are a cash-poor 25-year-old in your first full-time job and that one of your goals is to travel the world. On the way to work one morning you see an advertisement for volunteers to help new immigrants adjust to life in Canada. If you are clear that the main reason you want to travel is to learn about and experience other cultures, then you may decide to follow up on the ad. You might look at it as a great way to learn more about other cultures and to help someone else at the same time.

How is this different from what you would do if you weren't clear about your goals and weren't surfing for opportunities? First, you noticed the ad. As you clarify what you want, ways to get there will begin to manifest themselves in your life, and opportunities will make themselves known to you. People will hear you talk about what you want, and they will bring opportunities to you. You will think about what you want and see opportunities that you never noticed before. Second, once you spot these opportunities, you will be able to make quick decisions about whether to pursue them. You won't have to spend precious time internally debating each option; you will be ready to make a decision. In the end, you may ride a number of different waves that don't necessarily deliver you to the beach of your dreams, but each wave will bring you closer. You'll be confident that you are heading in the right direction as you surf for opportunities and head towards the shore.

Making It Happen: Creating a Personal Treasure Map

Representing your goals in a visual format is often a very useful way to help yourself internalize and manifest your desires. Personally, until I can visualize an image of something in my mind, whether it's earning a higher income, losing 10 pounds or publishing my book, I am not ready to achieve it. Visualization is often the signal to myself that I really do believe in my goal and am ready and willing to turn it into reality.

The actual visualization doesn't need to be a technically accurate representation of what you plan to accept into your life, it merely needs to be representative and believable. For example, I've always done well with attracting money into my life, and one of the images I like to picture is money in the mailbox. I imagine an envelope of money coming to me in the mail. You may laugh, but this visualization has worked for me many times. During university, money showed up in the form of unexpected scholarships, a small inheritance and a few government tax rebates. Currently, as an entrepreneur, my income always arrives by way of a cheque in the mail. No wonder I enjoy opening my mail every day.

Representing your dreams and goals visually usually brings them closer to fruition. An easy way to start your journey towards financial success, and the life success that it can enable, is to create a personal treasure map. To do this, gather up a bunch of old magazines, scissors, glue, a large piece of cardboard or construction paper and a cup of your favorite brew. Nothing fancy is required.

Now think about what you want to accomplish during your life. Maybe jot down a few notes on things that come to mind or reread the "Where Are You Headed?" section of this chapter. Then, with your favourite music playing in the background, and possibly a close friend who wants to create a treasure map of her own, you can get started. Flip through the magazines, cutting out words and images that strike you as good representations of what you wish to achieve in your life. For instance, when I created my treasure map specifically depicting what I wanted to accomplish through writing this book, I cut out the words "stargazer" and "strength and strategy." I added pictures of a woman making a speech and feet travelling down a garden path (representing my personal journey). I added quotations from Nelson Mandela and Darwin Kingsley about achieving things that seem impossible, and I listed the names of people who were supporting me in this project.

What images do your goals bring to mind? Spend an hour or two flipping through the magazines and cutting out pictures and words that represent what it is that you would like to have manifest itself in your life. Paste these images onto the construction paper and add any ideas or thoughts that are not visually represented. Then post your treasure map in a prominent place. Look at it often, dream about your vision for the future and be reminded of your larger objectives as you go about your day-to-day life. Or keep it in a private place, but refer to it often in order to remind yourself, visually and mentally, where you are headed.

You may think this is hokey, but I've done it numerous times and have found it to be helpful. Not only does it help you get in touch with what it is that you want in life, but it helps you focus on the goals you've decided are most important and avoid getting distracted with less meaningful activity.

Once you have completed your treasure map, summarize your most important life goals. These goals can be relationship goals, work goals, spiritual goals, health goals or any other type of goals that might be important to you. They will set the stage for the development of your specific financial goals, which will be dealt with in Chapter 5.

My Life Goals

Today's date: ____________________

Relationship Goals	
Work Goals	

Spirituality/ Emotional Goals	
Health Goals	
Other Goals	

3

Learning from Mom and Dad

Mama exhorted her children at every opportunity to "jump at de sun." We might not land on the sun, but at least we would get off the ground.

ZORA NEALE HURSTON

BELIEVE, THEN ACHIEVE

What you believe about money, consciously and unconsciously, is the most important factor in determining whether or not you are financially successful in life. Unless you believe you can achieve your financial goals, unless you believe you are worthy of your goals and unless you believe your goals are morally acceptable, you will have trouble achieving your financial objectives.

Until you are clear about what you really believe about money, and until you have unearthed all of your hidden childhood teachings about money, you are likely to have negative internal beliefs working against your financial desires. Whether taught explicitly or conveyed implicitly through the actions of your role models and society in general, your childhood lessons about money have a huge impact on your financial affairs.

Common beliefs with which many women are raised often include the following: "Rich people are sinful"; "Your husband will provide for you"; "The love of money is the root of all evil." Do these statements sound familiar? They do to many of us because we were taught to believe them. But are they really true? In reality, many rich people use their money to contribute to society, many women are not financially supported by husbands and money can be a wonderful enabler in the pursuit of positive goals. If we really look at our own thoughts about money and consciously choose what we want to believe, then we can build healthy financial attitudes and move closer and closer to personal prosperity.

Among the women I've interviewed with regard to determining their financial wealth, financial attitudes and beliefs learned in childhood were clearly just as important as was the ability to earn. Over the course of my interviews, I met a medical doctor with a negative net value, a nurse who has saved over $200,000, and a business manager worth under $50,000. One ambitious woman, with only a high school education and a salary of under $25,000 per year, owns twelve rental units in three separate apartment buildings. Clearly, these examples demonstrate that education and employment status are not the only indicators of how much wealth you can accumulate, nor are they always the most important. The real determining factor is your attitude.

If, after reading this chapter, you identify some hidden beliefs about money and begin to work towards changing the ones that are self-defeating while reinforcing the ones that are positive then this will be the most valuable chapter of the book. Changed attitudes lead to changed behaviour.

Father Knows Best?

So let's go back to the source. You start to learn about money directly or indirectly from your family of origin. Whether you realize it or not, you have heard and observed positive and negative messages about money every day of your life. For the vast majority of people, the messages parents convey are particularly influential in shaping their adult financial behaviour. Whether you act just like them (the most common situation) or rebel against their extreme behaviour, your parents' financial attitudes and actions become your frame of reference in adulthood.

LEAVE THE ROMANCE AT THE MOVIES

Let me illustrate with Alice's story. Alice is an intelligent, well-educated physician whose finances are, frankly, a mess. Although well-educated and determined, Alice has consistently worked against herself when it comes to money. Her history and current financial situation are described in detail in order to paint as full a picture as possible of the linkage between upbringing and recurring poor financial decisions.

Alice's parents divorced when she was young; her father did not provide child support. Her mother struggled financially, job-hopping while trying to raise three children on her own. As Alice puts it, "My mom did odd jobs along the way, she had a Grade 10 education and one year of secretarial training. Her outgoing personality helped, but overall, she just scraped by. She charmed her way into many different jobs, but often ended up quitting to follow men she was romantically involved with or to get away from them once the romance faded."

I asked Alice what she felt she had learned from her parents about money. She responded, "My dad was fairly frugal, my mother was not. Once he left, when I was nine, I saw everything through my mother's eyes and, unfortunately, learned my money management habits from her.

"My mom has never had more than two nickels to rub together. Some of it was hard times for sure, but even when she did have a few bucks, she didn't save. One Christmas she wasn't even able to save money for Christmas presents. Another time, when she split up with my first stepfather, she used her divorce settlement to buy furniture and a car. Then it was gone. She didn't have a pension or any savings.

"At that point, I decided to pursue medicine instead of teaching as a career. I was in high school and had heard that teachers' salaries weren't that good, and I guess I got scared. I didn't need to be rich, but I wanted to have some security. I didn't want to live like my mom."

Alice's mother clearly believed the old adage "Your husband will provide for you," and she abdicated responsibility for managing her own career and money wisely. When her father left, Alice, on the other hand, internalized the belief that you cannot rely on a man for financial support; instead, she pursued a high-paying career. However, Alice still does not manage her income wisely. Unfortunately, although she didn't want to live the way her mom did, in many ways she still does.

When you aren't clear about money you sabotage yourself. Money always seems to be a struggle. You want to ignore it, but the more you ignore it, the more it rears its ugly face. You never seem to have enough. Money gives you grief. If only you had more. So you focus on the money instead of on what is really creating your money problems – your beliefs, which drive your actions, which create your money problems.

Alice's self-sabotage was evident from the beginning of adulthood. In one instance, she left medical school for a year to follow a boyfriend to a new city. When she moved, she failed to have her credit card bills forwarded and damaged her credit rating by not paying them promptly. She ended up with no credit cards at all for the next few years, and restoring her credit was no easy task.

She explains, "When I graduated from medical school I tried to get a Visa card. It was almost three years later and I went to a bank to apply. The woman I talked to actually laughed at me. She said, 'I'm sorry, there is no way with your credit history.' I was so embarrassed. She completed the humiliation with, 'Just forget it. It will be years before you can get any credit.' Years later I finally did get a Visa, but I sure would have liked to have avoided all that grief along the way."

Alice was off to a rough start. Just like her mother, she placed following a man ahead of her career. Furthermore, she chose to disrespect her own financial health by not bothering to understand what she was getting into credit-wise and by being careless about her financial obligations. Subconsciously, Alice may have actually considered her actions to be noble. While she was ready to accept that she couldn't rely on others for financial security, she was not ready to "abandon" her mother by acting differently with regard to how she managed her money.

When you have unhealthy money attitudes you rationalize your behaviour with seemingly positive motives: You aren't rebelling against your parents; you're acting just like them – a show of support. You're letting your boyfriend show you he cares by letting him take care of you financially. But, in the end, you aren't taking care of yourself.

Alice continues: "After that I was good for about a year and a half. I just charged something and then paid it off. I was making really good money and if I racked up $4,000 of debt one month, I could pay it off quickly. I was proud of myself and I thought, 'This way I'm going to get Air Miles, too!' I thought I was saving somehow, getting something extra.

"I kept telling myself I would put money away for RRSPs, but it was hard enough to scrape together money for taxes each quarter. I thought, 'What am I doing wrong?' And yet I also thought I just needed this one more thing to complete the whole look in my apartment and then I could stop. And there it was. I rationalized it thinking, 'I can't pass this up, it's even on sale – a full year until I have to start making payments and no down payment – that's like money in the bank! And I can surely afford it by next year.'

"The next year I ended up moving to Ontario. Now I had all of this furniture to transport. So I was winding down in B.C. and spending money moving at the same time. In Toronto, work was slow to pick up at first. For the first three months I was barely making enough to cover my living expenses, and I actually went a few months without car insurance. When I was finally quoted $4,000 per year for car insurance, I gave up my car."

Why does Alice make these poor financial decisions? Much of it is obviously tied to her parents' behaviour. Both of Alice's parents have acted irresponsibly financially: her mother spent impulsively and never planned for the future, her father abandoned his financial responsibility towards his children. Although her father was fairly financially secure and fiscally prudent, subconsciously Alice sees him in a negative light. Thus, she likely associates having financial security with being uncharitable. At the same time, Alice has repeated many of her mother's poor money management habits. She spends impulsively and has neither set financial goals nor planned for the future. Even her frequent moves, following in her mother's "let's move on" pattern, have had costly financial implications. As a result, Alice sabotages her own opportunities for financial security.

Alice said it herself: "I had all these romantic attachments,"she states in reference to her impulsive purchases. Romantic maybe, but also foolhardy. Like her mother, Alice disregards sensible investments like a home because she fears being tied down and because it is unromantic. Would there have been any romance in spending time in jail if she had gotten into a car accident without insurance?

The good news is that Alice is only 32 years old, she has a solid career, and she has begun to realize that she is sabotaging herself financially. She is making a concerted effort to become better educated about money and wants to change. She has begun to face up to her situation honestly. The key element in her financial recovery will be her ability to become consciously aware of the forces that are causing her to fail because, in their current unconscious form, these forces are able to retain their power. Once Alice is clear about her negative attitudes, she can work to replace them with positive, consciously selected thoughts and can begin to base her actions on the latter. If she does this, then I have no doubt that her efforts will pay off. You can do the same, using the exercise at the end of this chapter, but first let's contrast Alice's situation with those of more financially successful women.

Alice's financial attitudes and decisions are the antithesis of the thinking and behaviour exhibited by the most financially successful women I interviewed. Many of these women were taught useful money values. Instead of seeing long-term investments as tying them down, they were taught that saving leads to more freedom in life. Their parents taught them that having money in the bank, so to speak, provides peace of mind, which is far more valuable than frivolous spending. None of these women feels deprived, and most of them have a few select spending priorities upon which they spend guiltlessly. At the same time, they make daily conscious decisions not to spend on non-priority items, and they feel proud of these decisions.

Save for a Sunny Day

In many ways Inez's story is typical of financially successful women. A 46-year-old municipal director, Inez has never married, owns her own home outright and has a net worth of over $300,000. When I asked her about her attitudes towards saving and investing, she had this to say: "Well, I was brought up to be a big saver so I probably save too much! My parents really instilled that in me. Growing up, we got an allowance and we were allowed to decide how much to save, but we were expected to save something.

"I can remember a sweater that I wanted so badly. I think I was in fifth grade. I really wanted this sweater, so my mom said she would pay half if I paid half. I remember wanting that sweater, saving for it, and buying it. I remember the day we went and bought it. Oh God, it was like heaven! I just thought it was so great and I wore and wore and wore that sweater. So you see, it instilled this lesson in me about saving, and then achieving the reward, and then appreciating the reward for a long period of time. I still love that sweater. I could still describe it to you. Those types of experiences really burnt themselves into my mind and guide my actions today."

Inez learned to enjoy anticipating the eventual sweet rewards that saving could deliver, whereas Alice was taught that money might as well be spent now because it always ends up running out sooner or later.

Inez continues: "I've always saved money and I have very painless ways of doing it. I plan a lot. I have all these automatic deductions so I don't see the money. I'm quite disciplined, and even if I saw the money, I wouldn't generally spend it. But I just find it so painless this way. My earnings go off to various investments and accounts. I have an account to save for this and an account to pay this off, and so on. For example, I have an account where I put a certain amount of money away for my house so that if any repairs need to be done I have money to pay for them. I don't have to ever go into debt. I hate debt.

"It's the way I want to live. It's choosing what you want to do and knowing why you chose it, instead of saying, 'Oh, I spent all my money. I wish I didn't do that.' If you want to spend all your money that's okay, but know that that's what you decided to do."

This is critical. We can all choose what we believe and how we act. People who are financially secure choose to make managing their money a priority, and they take actions in various areas of life to support this choice. They work towards obtaining well-paying jobs. They spend selectively. They take the time to learn how to manage their investments. They take the time to envision their future and to determine their monetary goals. They make choices; you can too, if you want to.

When you're clear and healthy about money, you enjoy saving. Saving leads to enjoyable purchases, provides security and gives you choice. You feel great when you decide not to purchase something you don't really want because you know you've reserved the option to enjoy the money you've saved in some other way, on some other day.

Sandra provides another inspiring example of a woman who has managed her finances extremely well. Her parents' values of financial self-sufficiency and frugality had a definite impact on Sandra's financial success.

A clinical psychologist worth over $2,000,000, Sandra describes her childhood this way: "I grew up in a small town in Alberta. My parents were both from Denmark. I am the oldest child and first generation born in Canada, which, I think, is a really critical factor in all of this. My parents were the only two individuals from their own families that came to Canada, so we didn't have any relatives in Canada. I learned from a very young age that there was no extended family to rely on and that I was pretty much on my own.

"I started working at the library when I was in Grade 6. By the time I was in junior high I was responsible for buying my own clothes. My parents provided food and the necessities, but I bought anything else I wanted. My father had his own distributing business and we weren't poor, but we weren't wealthy either. At the same time, it was expected that I would buy things for myself.

"Both of my parents thought debt was bad. This was made very clear to me when I was going away to university and I bought some Samsonite luggage on credit. They were appalled. It wasn't an outrageous amount to spend, it was certainly something that I could deal with, but it was not seen as a good thing."

Sandra went on to break her parents' rule about avoiding debt but generally only for investments. She has taken a very active role, through adulthood and in both of her marriages, in managing her own investment portfolio and in maintaining financial self-sufficiency. Certainly, Sandra's parents' example of careful financial management was not lost on her.

When you're healthy about money you don't want to hand the reins over to your partner when you enter a new relationship. You want to stay involved. You enjoy being involved. You may want to make joint financial decisions, but you always want to be involved because being involved is your responsibility to yourself.

Healthy Mind, Healthy Money

Even if your role models didn't exhibit ideal behaviour, it doesn't mean you can't surpass their performance. It may be harder to learn good financial attitudes and techniques later in life, but it is certainly not impossible. The first step is recognizing what you have learned about money. By reviewing and revising ill-fitting beliefs you will take an important step towards enhancing your own prospects for prosperity.

Making It Happen – Taking an Attitude Inventory

Take some time to identify the key messages about money that you learned from your parents and other key childhood influences. This will help you understand which messages are positive and need to be reinforced and which are holding you back and need to be altered.

In the space below, list all of the strong messages you received about money. Once you have finished listing these messages, check off whether you think each one has been helpful or unhelpful to you. I've provided some examples to get you started.

Messages I received about money as a child	Helpful	Not helpful
Talking about money is crass.		√
The love of money is the root of all evil.		√
Thinking about money is depressing.		√
Money should not be wasted.	√	
We've always been poor, that's just the way it is.		√

Once you have completed your list, select the unhelpful belief you most wish to change. Think of what someone who is really good with money would believe with regard to this topic and write an affirmation that counteracts the negative belief. For instance, if the unhelpful belief you selected is, "Talking about money is crass," then your affirmation might be: "It is healthy for me to learn more about money by talking to friends and financial experts about it. I am happy to openly discuss money." If you wrote, "The love of money is the root of all evil," then you might counter this with: "The amount of money a person has does not determine the quality of her heart," or "I can do as much good with my money as I choose to." You could also list the names of rich people who have done positive things with their money.

Each day, copy down your affirmation 25 times and look for examples of people who are living it. Put a copy of your affirmation in your wallet and anywhere else convenient. Each time you review your affirmation, spend a few minutes trying to visualize and feel what it would be like to truly live this belief.

You may find that doing this exercise brings up some strong emotions for you. That's okay. If this happens, then it means you are doing internal work that really needs to be done. Congratulations on having the courage to look within and feel your feelings. This is something that few people do, and yet only by truly examining your feelings about money and consciously deciding to change any destructive beliefs will you be able to move past them to more productive, abundance-generating thoughts.

When you are ready to change again, select another unhelpful belief from your list and repeat the process.

4

Balance, My Friend

Money is power, freedom, a cushion, the root of all evil, the sum of all blessings.

CARL SANDBURG

Now that you've begun to uncover the sources of your present-day attitudes towards money, let's take a look at where you are today. A balanced attitude towards money (and, indeed, towards most areas of life) is healthiest, but few of us learned the perfect balance in childhood. In other words, it makes for a happier life to believe that money is neither evil nor precious but, rather, a useful tool that helps you achieve your non-monetary goals. But how many people are actually that balanced in their view of money? In reality, many people feel conflicted about money.

THE BATTLE OF GOOD VERSUS EVIL

Darlene, a 64-year-old human resource consultant, exhibited a fair bit of internal conflict about whether money is good or bad during our interview. This, I believe, is one of the central money conflicts with which women struggle. Darlene first described her financial philosophy this way: "The universe is abundant. If you want something you can get it. It's deciding that is the key. If I have any reservation, it is about feeling deserving. What I find difficult is to not feel guilty.

"I think the feeling of security really comes from an inner peace that has nothing to do with money. At least ideally that's how it should be. At the same time, I can hear my mother saying, 'You don't want to be old without money.' There is a part of me that says, 'Hey, I don't really need a lot of money.' On the other hand there is a part of me that says, 'Well, Darlene, you like to live, you like to buy something every day, even if it is small.'"

Darlene wants to hold firm to her belief that the universe is abundant and will look after her, yet there is this nagging voice in the back of her head testing her faith. On one hand, she is struggling with a notion that pursuing money is somehow bad or greedy, while, on the other hand, she is acknowledging that she likes having money and living comfortably. Hence, her internal confusion and struggle continues.

Do you suffer from this same struggle between wanting to believe that the universe will provide for you and feeling concerned that it might not? The trick is to get to a place where you have balance: a mental space where you have faith that the future will be fine but where you are also an active participant in making it fine; where you aren't obsessed with earning and saving money but where you are fully conscious of your own finances and don't avoid dealing with them. A mental space where you instead educate yourself about money and are aware of the opportunities to build prosperity. And where you act on these opportunities, just as you act on appropriate opportunities in all areas of your life.

Yours, Mine and Ours

Another common area of conflict for women is relationships. Should you manage your joint finances together, or should you hand over responsibility for these to your partner? Relinquishing complete ownership for your own financial well-being is a dangerous trap to fall into – a lesson that many of the older divorced or widowed women I interviewed learned the hard way. Consider the advice of one such woman.

Janine, a 56-year-old real estate executive, started out in a traditional, the-man-controls-the-finances marriage. Now remarried to her second husband, she says, "The advice I give my daughters, who are 25 and 29, is from Day One to always save a portion of their money, to start RRSPs and to always plan for financial independence.

"If life brings you any other arrangement that's wonderful, but don't give up your financial independence. By financial independence, I mean being able to support yourself through your entire life and planning on doing that. I think this creates a greater feeling of security and, therefore, greater freedom in evaluating relationships without the extra baggage of worrying about how you would support yourself if you left. It's important not to surrender the financial part of your life to a relationship or anything else."

Many of the attached younger women I talked to felt conflicted about taking responsibility for and control over their own financial fortunes. On some level they believed that exerting their influence and power in their financial affairs somehow took away from their commitment and belief in the longevity of their relationships. If this sounds like you, give this belief a long, hard look. Discussing money and ensuring you are financially protected isn't unromantic. It's realistic. Not talking about such a key matter isn't a reflection of trust in the other party, it's simply putting your head in the sand and hoping for the best. This is not to say that your partner may not be better at, or more interested in, managing the details of your joint finances, but it makes sense to stay informed about your financial situation and to understand what is happening with your money – your future security. The key is balance – not being obsessed with money and financial security but not ignoring it either.

Nadine, a senior banking executive who works with high net-worth individuals, expresses the attitude she thinks women should have towards money: "Women should manage money and not let money manage them. Really that means avoiding extremes when it comes to money – not being overly frugal and not being a spendthrift either. My personal philosophy is that every day of life is wonderful and to deny yourself completely is to not fully enjoy something that may never come your way again. On the other hand, I think that you should be realistic and have a sound financial plan for emergencies and for retirement. A realistic, moderate approach to spending is probably best."

Consider the following ranges of beliefs about money. Where are you on each continuum? Are you happy with where you are? Are you in the middle on these continuums or at an extreme? You may find your beliefs are in conflict. Mark an X to show where your current beliefs fall on each continuum. Place a Y where you would like them to fall.

I don't want to think about money.	Money is a useful tool.	I am obsessed with money.

Someone will take care of me.	Being able to take care of myself enhances my relationships.	I look out for number one.

All work and no play	Sensible spending and spending priorities	Instant gratification

Concern over saving for the future means I'm not trusting the universe to provide.	I can be responsible about money and still have faith in a higher power.	The only thing that determines my prosperity is me.

People with money are greedy and corrupt.	Whether or not someone has money doesn't determine the state of her heart.	People with money are superior and I envy them.

Add a few continuums of your own if you like.

What came to mind while you were doing this exercise? Are there areas where you are strongly entrenched at the end of a continuum? If so, then what can you do to shift to a healthier position? Affirmations are one tool for change. Awareness helps as well. For deeply lodged issues you may even wish to consider talking to a therapist. More likely though, educating yourself with the information in this book, and making attitude and behaviour changes one step at a time, will start you moving in the right direction.

Making It Happen – Attitude Transfers

Attitude transfers work by consciously shifting some of the things you do really well in one area of your life to an area in which you are less successful. This is how it is done.

First, pick an area of your life in which you feel very successful and confident. Write down all of the positive beliefs you have about this subject in the left-hand column, under "Success Area Beliefs." In my hypothetical example below, I have selected relationships with co-workers as the area of success. Alternatively, you might focus on your ability as a parent, wife or friend; or your skill in a hobby such as photography, writing, cooking or sports.

Once you have finished making your success-area belief list, use the right-hand column to translate these positive beliefs into positive affirmations for a less successful area of your life. For our purposes, you should focus on money beliefs.

If you are like most us, then you will be amazed at how easy it is to write down positive beliefs relating to a component of your life that you believe is an area of strength. It may surprise you that it feels much more unnatural to write down the corresponding positive statements for an area of weakness. This demonstrates how important our beliefs are in determining whether we succeed in something or not. The relative level of discomfort you feel with regard to individual new money statements highlights the places where you have the most work to do on changing your thoughts.

Regularly read, repeat and recopy the affirmations on the right-hand side of the chart until they become internalized.

Sample Attitude Transfer

Relationships with Co-Workers Beliefs	Corresponding Money Statement
• I will always be able get along well with my co-workers.	• I will always have sufficient money.
• I am able to set clear boundaries with my co-workers and have no trouble saying "No" to taking on more than my share of the work.	• I can say "No" to purchases I don't really need or want because I know I have other priorities for my money.
• People enjoy working with me and I am a highly valuable team member.	• I enjoy managing my money and I am good at it.
• I love getting to know new people.	• I love learning more about money.
• There are many good jobs with pleasant work environments available to me at all times.	• There are many opportunities for me to improve my finances that are available to me at all times.
• I have clear ideas as to what kind of work environment will make me happy and can easily determine if a job is right for me.	• I have a clear idea of my financial plans and know what type of investments and expenditures

My Attitude Transfer

Success Area Beliefs	Corresponding Money Statement

You are now well on your way to solidifying the foundation of good money management – developing the right attitudes and beliefs. Next, we'll move on to setting appropriate goals and the basic principals of handling your money on a day-to-day basis.

5

Money Isn't Everything, But It Is Something!

I've been rich and I've been poor. Believe me, honey, rich is better.
SOPHIE TUCKER

It's time to start translating your new and improved prosperity beliefs into behaviour; success requires both thought and action. Developing an awareness of what you believe about money and its influence on your self-esteem and life experience is the first step. Reshaping your money thoughts, by clarifying what you believe about money and working to shift those beliefs to higher ground, provides the groundwork for prosperity. Action, in the form of acting on the opportunities for prosperity in your life and using your money effectively, completes the prosperity equation. We will begin our work on the action section of the prosperity equation by setting financial goals.

GOALS THAT SUIT YOU

When you set financial goals they need to be consistent with your non-monetary life goals. If the two are not compatible, then you will be in a constant state of internal struggle and frustration. Remember, money is the enabler to help you to achieve your life goals, not vice versa.

Each woman I met while researching this book placed a different level of importance on money. Some wanted to amass millions, while others were comfortable living below the poverty line. The key to contentment is clarity about, and compatibility between, the way you interact with your money and your overall life priorities, whatever those priorities may be.

Barbara, a part-time artists' model and language instructor, values her personal time much more than she does material non-necessities. Her financial situation reflects this. In her fifties, Barbara has raised three children primarily on her own but has never worked at a full-time, conventional job; instead, she focuses on minimizing her material needs. She lives in a very modest home, which she owns, and spends most of her time reading and writing. While her income falls below the government-defined poverty level in most years, she is able to maintain control over her time, which she considers to be precious. Her financial goals fit her life goals and meet her most pressing needs.

Others, like 34-year-old Ellen and her husband, consider it very important to save as much as possible early on in life so as to have greater freedom in later years. As she puts it, "We are very, very careful about what we buy and how we invest our money. If it means we don't go on holidays each year or that we go without new furniture for a few years, that's okay, we're happier that way. We feel comfortable knowing we are working towards our financial goals.

"When we got married my husband didn't share this attitude. He had worked in a family business where the business sort of supports you and you don't worry about saving. When we got married though, I made sure we started saving in a big way. We used our savings to buy a house and paid it off in four years. It was our overriding financial focus at the time. We've now moved up to a larger home and are working hard to get it paid off. At the same time, now that we've started a family our financial situation gives me the flexibility to stay at home and be a full-time mom. It's a great pay-off from all of those early years of frugality."

To Ellen, money represents freedom from stress. She puts it this way: "When you have enough money in the bank, when you have that security, it makes you freer to choose what you want to do in life. For instance, if you just can't stand your job you can quit. And even if you don't quit, having the financial option sets you free. It just gives you more stability overall. Money problems aren't wearing on you."

Buy Yourself Some Freedom

Money can buy you a measure of freedom. If you have savings, then you have more freedom to turn down those things you don't want in your life and to take advantage of those opportunities you do want. You are more likely to be able to say "No" to a job you don't like or to a relationship that isn't working. If you have your financial house in order, then you are more likely to be able to say "Yes" to a dream travel opportunity that arises out of the blue or a steal-of-a-deal antique hutch you stumble across. Most of all, even if you never need to, or choose to, fall back on your nest egg, you will have the psychological freedom to think about your options in life more broadly and to worry less about setbacks. Regardless of whether or not you consider material possessions to be important, you should not underestimate the psychological value of savings. A little moderation now can create a lot of freedom later.

Planning Your Journey

In Chapter 2 you defined your life's mission and set some long-term goals. Now it is time to get more specific. Working back from your overall vision for your life to your five-year and 20-year goals will help you to determine precisely what it is that you need to do now if you want to reach those goals.

In the chart below you can see how Marva, from Chapter 2, translated her long-term goals into short-term goals:

My Goals	Life Goals	5-Year Goals (Age 33)	20-Year Goals (Age 48)
Relationships	To have my own family and maintain a close circle of friends	Be in a committed long-term relationship	Have a family of my own and a close circle of friends
Work	To own my own retail business	Work in a retail management position	Own my own retail business
Spirituality	To have a balanced lifestyle with time for spiritual growth and physical exercise	Explore alternative spiritual beliefs Meditate regularly	
Health		Weigh 140 pounds or less Exercise 3 times per week Run at least one race per year	Exercise at least 3 times per week
Other	To own my own home and have enough retirement income to maintain a comfortable lifestyle and travel occasionally To explore and experience different cultures	Buy my own home Travel to Asia	Have my home paid off Have visited at least six foreign countries

What are your goals in life? What are your key values and priorities? What do you most wish to achieve?

Copy your life goals from Chapter 2 into the chart below. Then add 5-year goals, 20-year goals and the age you will be at each goal deadline.

My Goals	**Life Goals**	**5-Year Goals (Age:)**	**20-Year Goals (Age:)**
Relationships			
Work			
Spirituality			
Health			
Other			

Translating Dreams into Reality

To be meaningful, your financial goals need to be aligned with your long-term life goals. A financial goal of amassing $250,000 in the next five years is probably not in sync with attending art college and travelling the world during the same time period.

One key question concerns how much money you need to achieve your life goals. With retirement, for example, financial advisors use your age, estimated number of years to retirement, an estimated savings growth rate and an annual inflation rate to calculate the total amount of money you need. Some models are more sophisticated, but they all basically come to the same conclusion: you need a really large amount of money to retire. Personally, I think seeing and hearing these seemingly unachievable numbers is counterproductive for most people. I mean, why even bother trying to save if you have trouble putting away $50 each week and you supposedly need $2,000,000 to retire! The fact is, if you can pay off your home and contribute half of the maximum amount allowed to your RRSP each year, then you will have a comfortable retirement. If you do this, you will have accomplished more than most Canadians. Additional savings are gravy and may make retirement more fun, but you needn't stay up nights worrying about them.

Don't get me wrong, I think saving for retirement and for the achievement of other life goals along the way is very important, but, if you are just starting out in terms of building your finances, then I suggest you initially focus on developing the basic habits of saving money. For example, you could work towards a short-term goal of saving $2,000 over the next 12 months for a computer purchase. To do this you would have to save an average of $5.48 per day, or $166.67 per month. Then, once you've achieved this goal, you can move on to a larger goal, such as saving $5,000 in your RRSP account over the next two years and so on.

ONE STEP AT A TIME

Learning to manage your money is like learning to run. A marathon runner starts running the same as all the rest of us, by putting one foot in front of the other. I started running three years ago with a goal of running for 15 minutes, three times a week. I worked my way up in additional five-minute increments. Now I regularly do hour-long, 10-kilometre runs and recently ran my first race. Maybe one day I'll run a marathon, but that's not what I was thinking about when I self-consciously gasped and sweated my way along the boardwalk during those first few months of running. Starting to build your financial health is just the same. It may feel awkward and painful in the beginning, but the most important step is starting, and the best way to run the marathon – or to retire with $1,000,000 – is to put one foot in front of the other and get going.

Focus on Your Minimum, Not on Your Maximum

Once you get to the point where saving regularly feels comfortable, and you feel at ease with the basic mechanics of investing (all covered in later chapters), then you can start focusing on some longer-term, more challenging financial goals. For instance, you may set some rather significant retirement savings goals. When you do this though, you should consider what the minimum you'd need to retire is and set that as your minimum monthly savings target rather than calculating a large "nice-to-have/travel-around-the-world-when-I-retire"goal and missing it every month.

Advisors who say you need $1,000,000 or $2,000,000 to retire comfortably are using scare tactics. They are making assumptions that are unrealistic for the vast majority of us. They often assume, for instance, that you need a retirement income that is 70 percent of your pre-retirement income and that you provide that entire income from your own savings. But, if you've been careful enough to pay off your mortgage by the time you retire, do you really need an income equal to 70 percent of your pre-retirement income to enjoy retirement? Once you retire, you will no longer need to save for retirement, you should own most of the possessions that you need and you are unlikely to still be supporting children. You will no longer be contributing to the Canada Pension Plan (CPP), the Quebec Pension Plan (QPP) or Employment Insurance, and you won't have work-related expenses like parking and work clothes. I believe you can manage just fine on 50 percent of your gross pre-retirement income if you don't plan to create significant additional living expenses by, for example, taking long, exotic trips.

Another thing about those scare tactic numbers is that they are expressed in tomorrow's dollars. In other words, the dollars required are expressed in terms of how much money you will need 10 or 20 years down the road, with 10 or 20 years of inflation built in. To look at it another way, we all know that you would need a lot more than $10 today to buy what you could have bought 20 years ago with $10. In quoting numbers like $1,000,000 and $2,000,000 of required retirement savings, people are often stating the amounts they think you will need 20 years from now, assuming that $1,000,000 or

$2,000,000 will buy a lot less in 20 years than it will now. I prefer to express figures in today's dollars, which are much easier to relate to than are tomorrow's dollars.

Furthermore, even though government social benefits are eroding and can be expected to continue to erode, I have no doubt that, as a retiree, you will have some government contribution to your income, particularly if you are in financial need. Today's senior citizens are eligible for Old Age Security payments of approximately $5,000 per year once they turn 65. If they earned wages, then they are also eligible for CPP or QPP payments to a maximum of approximately $9,000 per year. The exact amount of CPP or QPP paid depends on how many years they worked and their salary. If they have very low retirement incomes, then they may also qualify for federal Guaranteed Income Supplements of up to $5,800 for a single pensioner and up to $7,500 for a couple.[1] So you can see that you really don't need to plan to save all of your retirement income yourself.

To give you a basic idea of what you should be saving for retirement each month, I have created an information table based on your current age. The figures in it represent what you would have to save each month, starting this month, in order to generate supplemental monthly retirement income from your investments that is the equivalent of $1,000 in today's dollars. In other words, the table states the amount you would have to save each month from now until you are 65, such that a month after you turn 65 you can withdraw a sum of money that will allow you to purchase roughly what you can purchase with $1,000 today. Then each month after that, until you turn 80, your accumulated savings would allow you to withdraw that same amount of money.

The specific assumptions used to build this table are as follows:

1. You retire at age 65 and live to age 80. I've made this assumption because 65 is still a typical retirement age for people, and the average life expectancy for Canadian women is currently just under 80 years.
2. Your investments grow at seven percent per year. This is based on the assumption that you will invest your savings in a mixture of low-risk investments like Canada Savings Bonds and high-risk investments like stocks, following the strategies covered in the investment section of this book.

A seven percent return is fairly conservative compared to what most financial advisors use, but I'd rather underestimate than overestimate what you can earn from your investments.

3. Annual inflation of three percent. I've made this assumption based on the average long-term inflation rates in Canada. It is important in calculating the numbers because it tells us how much of your seven percent investment gain will be negated each year due to inflation versus how much your investments grow in terms of real purchasing power.
4. You are saving this money within your RRSP account and therefore are not taxed on it until you begin to withdraw money during retirement. The money that you take out during each month of retirement would only be taxable at that time.
5. The day you retire you buy a fixed term 15-year annuity (an investment that will pay you the same amount each month for 15 years) with your retirement savings. In other words, this table assumes that the day you retire you quit saving altogether and start spending your retirement savings. It assumes you withdraw the same amount from your retirement savings each month for the next 15 years.

Using the Table

Assuming you haven't saved any money yet, you can look up your current age in the first column and see how much you would need to save each month between now and your 65th birthday for every $1,000 worth of monthly retirement income you would like to have.

How do you decide how much personal savings-funded retirement income is appropriate? Well, here are some guidelines that I think are sensible. According to actuary Malcolm Hamilton,[2] the typical Canadian couple can count on the equivalent of approximately $25,000 in retirement income from government programs and tax breaks once they reach age 65. For a single person, whether single for her entire life, widowed or divorced, this figure is $15,000. (Keep in mind that some of these benefits are income-tested, which means that if you have other sources of retirement income then you may not receive as much as this from the government. Furthermore, as we all know, government programs are frequently altered, so the longer you have until retirement, the less likely the programs in place today will exist exactly as they are in their present form.)

Nevertheless, as a starting point, I suggest you use the table to get an idea of how much you should be saving for retirement. Decide what level of yearly income you think you could comfortably live on in retirement and then, depending on your marital status, subtract $25,000 or $15,000. Then divide this yearly amount by 12 to get a monthly figure. For example, if you are married and want a retirement income equivalent to $40,000 in today's money, then you would calculate $40,000 - $25,000 = $15,000. Fifteen thousand dollars divided by 12 months is $1,250 per month. You then look up the number next to your current age in the chart and multiply it by 1.25, since you want 1.25 times the $1,000 per month upon which the chart is based. This is the amount you and your spouse would have to save each month, starting now and assuming you don't currently have any retirement savings put away.

If, instead, you are single, 35 years old, have no retirement savings and want an extra $1,250 per month in retirement income over and above what the government provides, then you need to start saving $250 per month. This would provide you with a retirement income equivalent to $30,000 per year, including $15,000 from the government. You arrive at the $250 monthly savings figure by looking up age 35 in the table. There you can see that for every $1,000 in extra retirement income you need to save $200 per month. Since you want $1,250 per month, you need to save 1.25 times this amount, or $250 per month.

Estimate your own monthly savings requirements using the following information.

Age	$/Month	Age	$/Month	Age	$/Month
18	$85	34	$190	50	$560
19	$90	35	$200	51	$610
20	$95	36	$210	52	$675
21	$100	37	$225	53	$745
22	$105	38	$240	54	$830
23	$110	39	$255	55	$930
24	$115	40	$270	56	$1,055
25	$120	41	$285	57	$1,215
26	$125	42	$305	58	$1,415
27	$130	43	$325	59	$1,685
28	$140	44	$350	60	$2,060
29	$145	45	$375	61	$2,630
30	$155	46	$405	62	$3,575
31	$160	47	$435	63	$5,470
32	$170	48	$475	64	$11,155
33	$180	49	$515	65	$136,265

			Example:
My retirement annual income goal		________	$30,000
Minus government funding	-	________	- $15,000 (single)
My retirement income savings goal	=	________	= $15,000
	÷	12	÷ 12
My monthly retirement savings goal	=	________	= $1,250
	÷	1000	÷ 1000
Multiplier for table's monthly savings	=	________	= 1.25
Table's monthly savings	x	________	x $200 (age 35)
My monthly retirement savings goal	=	________	= $250 per month

More Table Lessons

The above exercise was designed to give you some ideas about what you want to save for retirement. Granted, it is less than perfect: it doesn't take into account what you might already own and it is based on specific assumptions, any one of which could be changed to produce different results. But it is useful. Now at least you have a number in mind.

The table itself also demonstrates a number of other important points. First, it clearly shows that the earlier you start, the more painless the whole process will be. If you start saving at age 30, then you only have to save about $155 per month in order to start collecting the equivalent of $1,000 worth of today's spending power the month after you turn 65. However, if you waited until the last possible moment, then the day you turn 65 and retire, you would have to come up with $136,265 to buy the annuity that would pay you back $1,000 per month for the next 15 years. Second, I hope that the table shows you that financial security in retirement is not out of reach. By talking about what you need in today's dollars instead of in future dollars you should have a better feel for what you need to save in figures that you can relate to.

Remember, it is achievable, and along the way having money saved will buy you an immense amount of freedom of choice – the greatest benefit of all.

If you already have retirement savings or want to calculate what you should be saving using different assumptions (say you want to retire at age 55 or want your retirement income to last 25 years instead of 15), then I suggest you use one of the many retirement calculators available on-line. You can start at any of the major Canadian banks' home pages and look under RRSP or retirement planning topic areas. These interactive calculators are easy to use and can often deliver individualized results with just a few minutes of effort.

DO THE NUMBERS ADD UP?

We've talked about retirement goals, but I am sure that you have other goals between now and retirement that have a financial component to them. Maybe you want to have your home paid off within 10 years or save $15,000 for your child's university education. The important thing is to try to make your financial goals specific in terms of when you want to achieve them and how much money is required. For example, a goal of saving $10,000 over the next two years is better than a goal of saving some money for a down payment on a house in the next few years.

Let's return to Marva. Her financial goals might look like this:

Financial Goals	5-Year Goals	20-Year Goals
1. Own my own home and have it paid off within 20 years	Have $10,000 saved for a down payment by Jan. 1, 2005 (This means adding at least $150 per month to my current savings.)	Make at least three double mortgage payment each year starting Jan 1. 2005
2. Travel to Asia	Contribute $75 per month to my travel fund starting this month	
3. Save for $1,000 per month supplemental retirement income	Save $140 per month in my RRSP	Continue saving the equivalent of at least $140 (in today's dollars) in my RRSP each month

Look back to your 5-year and 20-year life goals and try to create appropriate financial goals to match them. Write down your financial goals here.

Financial Goals	5-Year Goals	20-Year Goals
1.		
2.		
3.		

Building your financial worth is easier than you think. Once you get started, courage, commitment and patience are what you need to keep going. The chapters that follow will lay out all of the financial and investment information you need in order to manage your money wisely. The courage, commitment and patience to act on this information are yours to contribute.

THERE ARE NO LIMITS!

I'd like to close this chapter with the amazing story of a young woman who, in her twenties, controls over $1,000,000 worth of real estate. Natasha has essentially built her wealth on her own and has been extremely goal-oriented throughout her life.

Natasha's father was murdered when she was 10, and this experience left her highly determined, independent and driven. Natasha started her first business – a small publishing company and a teen drop-in centre – when she was 15. She bought her first house when she was 17. Currently married and 27, Natasha is the driving force behind her commercial property development company, which has just finished building a $1,600,000 retail complex in St. Albert, Alberta. Setting goals and working towards them has always been very important to Natasha.

"You have to set goals and write them down. I've always done this and once I got married I started doing this with my husband as well. My husband and I, together, wrote a list of 10 things we wanted to do when we first got married. My husband said, 'If we do one-quarter of these things, I'll be incredibly happy.' The goals were things like investing more money and travelling. Five years later, we have achieved all of the items on the list.

"For instance, one of our goals was to take a holiday together because we had never done that. My husband had never even been outside of B.C. and Alberta. So we put $600 down on a cruise that we could not afford. We didn't have any spare money for this, but we calculated that if my husband worked some overtime every week until the trip we could pay for it. So he started doing that, and I got some extra contract work, and we both worked night and day for two months. We were both dead tired and very crabby, but at the end we had the money for the cruise."

Natasha and her husband now own a small retail business, seven residential rental properties, five commercial spaces in their new building and their own home. All of these investments have been made based on setting goals and working towards them one day at a time, one step at a time.

As Natasha puts it, “I highly encourage people to write down their goals and then work to achieve them. Start one thing and then grow. A strong foundation is very important. Don’t get in over your head; just take one step at a time. There is no such thing as a million dollars overnight. It takes hard work and determination. Just keep going.”

And with that, I hope you just keep going with this book and continue to pursue your own financial goals.

6

A Bird in the Hand

I like to go to Marshall Field's in Chicago just to see how many things there are in the world that I do not want.

SISTER MARY MADELEVA

When you are clear about money and its role in your life it has no power over you; you have power over it. It is a tool you can use, and enjoy using, to enhance your life. You use it to provide security and to buy the things and experiences that are really valuable to you as you surf for opportunities. You feel good about all the things you choose not to spend it on. You feel proud of what you do and what you don't do with your money. As we move on to the second element of the prosperity equation – wasting less – you'll learn how to set spending priorities and to save money without sacrificing quality of life.

SUPER SAVERS VERSUS SLOPPY SPENDERS

Super savers share a genuine enjoyment of the process of saving money. They take pride in setting spending priorities and thrive on finding cost-conscious ways to get the things they want the most. They genuinely like the feeling of empowerment that goes with turning down the things they don't want. They like having the ability to take advantage of unexpected opportunities and make spur-of-the-moment spending decisions. For them, taking care of their money is a source of pride.

Sloppy spenders, on the other hand, frequently get bogged down, find it painful to try to climb out of debt and often end up trying to ignore the whole thing. As Dale, the owner of a market research firm, puts it, "It's kind of like my weight, I ignore it and pretend it's not there, but that doesn't solve anything."

When your relationship with money is clouded, you try to ignore it, but it keeps rearing its ugly head. Money problems keep coming back and draining your energy. You feel guilty about money, you feel powerless over money, you feel fed up with the whole thing and you want it to go away; but of course it won't.

It all relates back to the paradox. Weak money managers often think that saving money has to hurt, but super savers realize that the more you focus on saving early on, the more you will ultimately end up having to spend. They know they can save without making painful sacrifices because they know what they are willing to sacrifice and what they aren't willing to sacrifice. They know where their sacrifice boundaries lie. They know they can get what they want without spending their entire income each month and they know that their savings will buy them the chance to take advantage of opportunities that arise unexpectedly.

Balancing Faith with Realism

Laura, a 53-year-old minister, shares her experience of how mistakenly equating disregard for her money with faith has led to unnecessary financial woes and worries about her not-too-distant retirement.

Laura grew up in Ontario, the daughter of a salesman and a school-teacher. She was taught to view money as something to be enjoyed immediately. She explains: "Money was to be used to enable your life in the here and now. It wasn't something to possess and hang on to. You didn't need to plan for the future financially. The future was expected to take care of itself."

Laura absorbed her parents' attitude towards money. She felt that concerning herself with financial matters would, in a sense, be lowering herself. It would suggest she didn't trust in the universe to provide for her. Instead of learning to balance faith with realism, Laura learned to treat the money that flowed into her life sloppily. She acted almost contemptuously towards her money, giving little thought to achieving the experiences that she wanted for herself and her family without squandering her cash.

Laura's parents had done the same thing while Laura was growing up. The income Laura's mother earned was spent on luxuries, even though she earned more than Laura's father. Laura's parents believed the husband should be the primary breadwinner and never considered using the supplementary income to build financial security; instead, they were the first family on the block to have a dishwasher. They had a housekeeper and expensive hobbies.

Laura's father died in 1995, at age 87, leaving no insurance, no spousal pension and no sizable assets. Laura's 88-year-old mother lives on a modest teacher's pension in a rented apartment that she shares with Laura. Financially she gets by, but that's all.

As does the parent, so does the child – unfortunately. Laura exemplifies this statement. During her early adult life she followed her mother's footsteps into teaching, and she married and had two children with little thought to building any sort of nest egg. In 1977 she divorced, leaving her marriage with a three-year-old, a seven-year-old and a grand total of $2,000 to her name. She moved west and spent 15 months living with her brother and his family while she tried to gain her financial footing.

Laura struggled to find a way to support her children as a single parent. "My teaching qualifications were inadequate in B.C., so I took a job as a bank teller. It lasted about nine months." This was followed by nine months as a travelling sales representative and a few more months as an administrative assistant before she decided to go back to school.

"I thought I'd go and take whatever courses I had to, to go back to teaching. I'd just get student loans. I mean I had nothing anyway, so who cares, you know? So I applied and the university told me they wouldn't give me any credit for my Teacher's College training and years of teaching experience. I would have to do the whole four years to get my education degree. So I asked myself, 'Do I really want to be a teacher?'

"I decided to take a general degree and see where it led. Probably social work. Then while I was taking that degree, and getting more and more into debt, I decided I wanted to be in the ministry. It wasn't just out of the blue; I was active in the church. However, it meant I had to finish my bachelor's degree and then take three years of seminary."

It's obvious that Laura was not at all clear about her life goals during these early years as a single parent. It's no surprise, then, that she didn't have any specific financial goals either for the short-term or the long-term.

Shortly thereafter, Laura received an unexpected financial windfall. "In the middle of this, my former mother-in-law died and left my children quite a bit of money, about $160,000 each. It was left for their upbringing because their grandmother could see that her son was not taking care of them. He never gave us any child support, and so his mother cut him out of the will and left his share to the children. This meant all of our needs were looked after and I could go to school at my own pace and raise them, which, I convinced myself, was what she would have wanted me to do."

This is a point in Laura's life where she had a wonderful opportunity to build some long-term financial security for herself and her children. Unfortunately, she didn't see it that way, and her childhood learning about money prevailed. As Laura describes it, her parents believed that children should have the experiences they wanted regardless of the cost.

"My parents' attitude was that their children were so wonderful that they deserved whatever they wanted. My parents would usually buy us whatever we wanted even if they had to borrow the money to do so. It wasn't extravagant things; it was things for our development. If I wanted to have piano lessons I could have them. If I wanted to go to camp I could go to camp.

"The only thing that I never got, that I always wanted, was a horse. When my children inherited this money, guess what I did? I bought a horse. We had a great time for a year, but then my school studies picked up, the kids lost interest and we sold the horse. Of course, it was in a down period and nobody was buying a pleasure horse. So I donated it to a charity camp.

"I didn't think about priority trade-offs because I didn't want things like TVs; I wanted experiences, which seemed like a worthy goal to me. I wanted to take my children to the symphony and I wanted to take them on trips. I wanted them to have lots of good books around them. My daughter wanted to go to private school, so she went to private school. It didn't occur to me that she shouldn't go. If the money was there she should go.

"We lived a very good middle-class existence. To get money I just had to convince the trustees that whatever I wanted the money for was important. So the kids had a really good time. My son was a competitive skier and he got to go on all sorts of trips. I didn't have to take out any student loans, even though it took me quite a while to finish university. I was only going part-time because I was driving my son all over the country to these ski meets."

Laura's description of what she spent her children's money on shows a real disregard for their long-term financial health. Her motives were noble – she wanted them to have enjoyable learning experiences – but there are many much more cost-effective ways to provide positive learning experiences. Instead of buying books, they could have used the library. Instead of slowing her progress at university to drive her son to ski meets, she could have clarified whether her objective in driving him was to provide transportation or to spend time with her son. If it was to provide transportation, she could have carpooled with other parents; if it was to spend time together, she could have done so in a way that didn't mean she couldn't attend university. Horse camp instead of owning a horse, community group activities, church activities, co-operative efforts, low-cost adventures like camping – these are just a few of the ways Laura could have enriched her children's experience without spending a small fortune. While she concentrated on giving her kids positive experiences by spending on them, she deprived them of the gift of learning good money management habits by example; instead, both of her children, now in their twenties, have little or nothing left in their trust accounts nor do they own any hard assets.

Meanwhile, Laura is struggling to pay off her own debt, which peaked at $44,000 by the time she finished her studies. She hopes to have it paid off by the year 2001, at which point she will be 55. Laura knows she made some mistakes along the way and has begun to worry about retirement. It seems that for the first time she has begun to be conscious about money in her life.

"I only have until I am 65. We don't have a compulsory retirement age in the ministry, but I know I am going to be tired. I am already tired. So I've had to do a lot more thinking about that and try to plan for it. In the past, I always dismissed money as unimportant. If I had it that was great, and if I didn't that was too bad.

"I also tend to like expensive stuff. For example, when I was looking for a car a few years ago I just knew I had to have a Honda. It was all right if it was second-hand, but I had to have a Honda. I got a nice Honda Accord. Now I'm driving my mother's Taurus, but I just don't feel right in it. Yet, I don't make the kind of money that enables me to afford a Honda Accord. I have to change my attitude; but then I think, 'Well why should I? I deserve a Honda just like anyone else.'"

Laura's story really exemplifies the paradox of money. Money never had to become as important in her life and as stressful to her as it did. If she had paid attention to it when her children received the trust fund and had treated it with respect, then she could be in a very different financial situation now. The paradox for Laura is that money is now important for her in a negative way because she tried for so long to believe it wasn't important. She thought that if she paid any real attention to it, it would detract from her family's quality of life. And that's just not true!

Laura is now working to learn more about managing her finances and is trying to change her spending behaviour. She realizes the folly of her past spending habits. She explains, "I think I am basically a gregarious, open person. I think life is wonderful and worth living, and you don't need money to be okay because you don't need money to be okay as a person. However, I didn't look after my money carefully in the past because I didn't fully understand the other side of the equation: you still need money to live. I understand that now. My advice to others is save 10 percent of your income, and if you find that difficult, then go to therapy because you have a deep-rooted problem."

Laura is still having a tough time reconciling the notions of having financial security and being a good Christian. Until she is able to reconcile these beliefs, I think she will have a tough time turning her financial position around. Laura knows what to do, as her last comment suggests. The question is whether she will follow her own advice.

Pick Your Spots

Colette, the 48-year-old owner of a highly regarded communications agency in Toronto, represents the other side of the coin. Colette was the oldest of four and learned financial responsibility at a young age. Here, once again, the influence of family of origin plays a big role in how a woman manages her finances as an adult.

"My parents divorced when I was very young, so I learned quite young to be financially independent. When I was 11 years old, I was working in a concession booth in the park. When I was 13, I was working as a cashier in a supermarket. I said I was 16 so that I could work there. I had personal responsibility for myself from a pretty young age. I bought my own clothes throughout high school. I grew up understanding the value of financial independence.

"My mother supported us and she worked as an entrepreneur – nothing like your typical nuclear family of that era. We were one of the few families where there wasn't a mother and a father. In some ways it was hard, but in other ways it was a good grounding in terms of life. At the same time, my mother didn't have great money management skills, and I took on a lot of personal responsibility for providing for myself early on. In my family I watched people be irresponsible with money, so I think my carefulness with money is a reaction to the uncertainty and lack of security that went along with financial irresponsibility."

Colette reacted to the lack of certainty and control over money in her family of origin by taking firm control over her money as an adult. Colette is one of the most financially successful women I interviewed, and she shared her approach.

"The financial thread that runs through my behaviour is my understanding that if I put effort in, I get returns. Those returns mean financial independence and choice. For me money has always been very important. I think I have a deep fear of being poor. I never want to be in a position where I can't meet the financial responsibility to my own family. When I divorced, I was totally responsible for my children, and that's when this fear was most prominent.

"I've never had any debt. I've always been debt-averse. If I absolutely had to have a car or a home and didn't have the money I was willing to go into debt, but I would do everything I could to pay it off as quickly as possible. I didn't even have a credit card for the longest time, even though it was very unfashionable not to. There was a point where I was travelling so much for business that I finally had to have a credit card, but I made a point of never carrying a credit card balance owing from one month to the next.

"I paid my mortgage off within about five years of buying my house. I was always very focused and people would say to me, 'But it's very un-Canadian to do that!' My family would tease me and say, 'Everybody has debts, you're not very normal.' And I would reply, 'Well, so what.'

"I prioritized things differently. For me travel was always a big priority, so I would always make sure there was enough money for travel. And I learned to ski. I remember when I first started skiing I had a choice of either buying ski equipment or replacing the washing machine, and I made the decision to buy the ski equipment. So I wasn't absolutely, totally sensible."

Colette's decision to limit, but not eliminate, frivolous spending is central to her financial success. This is characteristic of women who do well financially.

Set Spending Priorities

Being able to save money consistently over the long haul is like eating wisely. In both cases, going on an austerity plan that drastically alters and limits your intake, whether we're talking about food or purchases, is bound to fail. That's where having some less restrained spending priorities comes in. If you are going to stay the course on healthy eating or healthy money management, then it helps to pick a few areas in which to loosen the reins. Just as you might allow yourself to consume peanut butter and bagels without guilt, so you might decide that travel and skiing are two areas in which you plan to financially indulge yourself. Of course, if you're practising healthy eating and healthy spending you're not going to binge uncontrollably in either of these areas, but you are going to enjoy your chosen pleasures without guilt.

Classifying an item as a spending priority doesn't mean that you don't look for savings. For example, if travel is one of your spending priorities, then you could still take advantage of free frequent-flier flights and link personal travel with business trips wherever it makes sense. If you enjoy travel and other cultures, then it's natural to have friends of other nationalities. By staying with friends and friends of friends in exotic locales you could save on accommodations. You could participate in a work-abroad program and look for travel deals and flight sales. Finding the best ways to stretch your travel budget is often just as much a part of the fun as the trip itself. The idea is not to spend extravagantly on your spending priorities but to build a reasonable amount of funding into your budget and then surf for available opportunities.

Spending priorities are important to intelligent lifelong budgeting. They are the things you can feel good about when you are skipping other enjoyments in order to be frugal. Having a positive near-term spending priority to keep in mind is what makes your savings restraint more palatable. It is a key contributor to keeping you on-track over the long run.

Good Habits Die Hard

Returning to Colette's story, she explains how she continued to follow her frugal spending philosophy even as an executive. "Over time I managed to do well and, eventually, to make quite a lot of money in business. What I always knew was that I wanted to have choice, that the only way I could have choice was if I was financially independent. I didn't want to have to go to a job that I hated every day. I didn't ever want to be in a position where I couldn't pay the mortgage, the rent or look after my kids the way they needed to be looked after."

Over time, Colette uncoupled her spending from her earnings. In other words, she followed her same sensible spending patterns regardless of whether her salary increased. Once the basic necessities of life and her spending priorities were covered, she saw the next most preferable use for her money to be saving and buying herself more and more freedom of choice for the future.

Colette's friends do not generally share her philosophy. "I don't think I am typical," she says. "I have a lot of friends who are my age, and they are usually in one of two categories. Some of them have never married, and they have spent their entire life spending what they make on clothes, cars and whatever. In many instances they don't have any real assets, and if I was them, I'd be absolutely terrified as I got older. The second category is friends who are just starting their families in their early forties. They've got 20 years of looking after kids and putting them through school ahead of them. So some of the things that appeared to be financial disadvantages in the past, you know, like having my children at a fairly young age, are now advantages. I have most of the expenses of life behind me, and I did it all frugally. Now I can take it easy."

Colette talked about being motivated to save by fear – fear of not having enough money to care for her children in bad times and fear of not having options to walk away from bad situations. These days a lot of modern psychology proclaims that we shouldn't be motivated by fear; instead, we should trust in the universe and live on faith. Personally, I think that the two are not incompatible and that fear can be a very positive motivator as long as it is not paralyzing. Sure, confront your fears, conquer your fears, but listen to them too. Some of them are really the voice of your own instincts or intuition talking to you. Some of them may just be asking you to be realistic and to have a back-up plan in uncertain times.

Colette continues: "I'm glad my fears of being trapped in a bad situation without choice have led me to live frugally and save. I don't think I've ever felt deprived. I feel great about how I've managed to do so much with my money and still accumulate a healthy net worth. The better I do, the more the fear is replaced with pride in what I've achieved and determination to continue to succeed. Without the initial fear and the savings it resulted in, I wouldn't have had the courage to leave the security of regular paycheques to start my own company. Thank God for rational fears!"

With early frugality come later rewards. Colette talks about her more recent spending: "Recently I make the decision to reward myself with a little, two-seater sports car. It was a totally frivolous, wonderful, fun thing to do, and I struggled with it. But I did it. Naturally, I paid cash. The guy at the car lot said to me, 'You should lease this, it should be a company car.' But I wasn't going to buy it unless I could buy it outright, so I just wrote him the cheque for it. I think he thought I was totally out of my mind!

"My sports car was a nice treat. It's probably the last big thing that I am going to buy. My focus now is on retirement and trying to put away as much money as I can, again so that I have choice."

All along Colette has believed that the peace of mind that comes from having savings is worth more than buying non-necessities along the way. Even now that she is on very solid financial ground, Colette still takes her splurges seriously. She remains fully conscious of how she is spending, and she understands that in every spending decision she is making a conscious choice between present-day consumption and future spending alternatives.

HERE'S A RECAP OF THE KEY PRINCIPLES OF SUCCESSFUL SAVERS:

1. **The Paradox:** The more you consider money unimportant and ignore it, the more attention you will ultimately have to pay to it when times are tough. Saving early means you will have to worry much less about money later; it buys future peace of mind.
2. **Balance:** Saving money is like eating wisely. Moderation is the key.
3. **Prioritization:** Everyone needs a few spending priorities on which money can be spent without guilt.
4. **Saving money can be fun:** Super savers know that the thrill of finding a great deal to get whatever it is that they really want is often as much fun as possessing the item itself. Keep a list of things you plan to buy in your wallet or in your mind. That way, when a great deal appears, you can act on it confidently, knowing you are making a good spending decision.
5. **Surf for opportunities:** Surfing for opportunities to maximize your enjoyment in your spending priority areas without blowing the budget can be a source of joy in and of itself.
6. **De-couple spending and income:** Basing your spending on what you need to live, rather than on what you earn, while keeping your spending comfortably below your income level, is a significant contributor to savings. De-couple your spending and income.
7. **Consciously choose between today and tomorrow:** Every spending decision is a decision between having something today and having the freedom of choice to have something else in the future.
8. **Buy yourself some freedom:** Make the decision to buy yourself the freedom to take advantage of future opportunities to say "Yes" to what you really want and "No" to what you don't want by building your own financial security.

Making It Happen -- Assessing Your Net Worth

In the next chapter you will design your monthly budget; however, first let's get a picture of where you currently are financially by completing your net-worth statement – a snapshot of your current financial position. Your net worth is the value of your assets minus any debts you have. It tells you what you would be left with if you sold everything you own and paid off your debt with the proceeds.

List all items of value that you own and their estimated market value (what you could sell them for today), and then list your debts. The difference between the two is your net worth. Measuring your net worth is a good place to start as you begin to get serious about the numbers.

Financial Assets:	$$$$$$$
Bank Account Deposits	______
Certificates of Deposit	______
Guaranteed Investment Certificates	______
Bonds	______
Mutual Funds	______
Stocks	______
RRSP Savings	______
Savings in Company Savings Plan	______
Pension Plan Vested Value (the amount that you would be paid in cash if you left your job today)	______
Other	______

Tangible Assets:	$$$$$$$
Real Estate	______
Vehicles	______
Home Furnishings	______
Jewelry	______
Art Work	______
Ownership in a Business	______
Other	______
TOTAL ASSET MARKET VALUE: (Add together the value of all of your assets)	______

Liabilities (Debts):	$$$$$$$
Store Card Debt	
Credit Card Debt	
Mortgage	
Student Loan	
Car Loan	
Other Bank Loans	
Personal Loans	
Other Amounts Owing	
TOTAL DEBT	
TOTAL ASSET VALUE - TOTAL DEBT =	
	THIS IS YOUR NET WORTH

7

Trimming the Fat

I glory
More in the cunning possession of my wealth
Than in the glad possession.

Ben Jonson

Everyone Can Save Something

At the end of this chapter you will develop your monthly budget, including not just what you plan to spend on, but also your planned monthly savings. If you are skeptical about having money left over for savings, then listen to the guidance Anne, co-owner of a chain of beauty salons, gives to her employees. "I coach my employees to save money to meet their long-term goals. When they are at a certain point in their income I insist that they start an RRSP and I do not let up until they do. I say, 'I recommend you save this much each month given your age and your income; however, I am not going to be so dictatorial as to insist that it be this much.' So, I've got kids making $1,500 a month – which is not a lot of money – putting $50 a month into an RRSP. Then I remind them from time to time that they should be increasing their contributions. If they really do not want an RRSP, I try to get them to save towards another end. I tell them, 'You have to protect your future, let's look at saving to buy a condo or a car. You should start getting some real assets to your name.'

"Another thing I am really on them about is not to amass ridiculous credit card debt. There have been a lot of employees who have come to me in a financial mess. I don't say, 'Get rid of all of your debt, and then start saving', because debt is something that is extremely difficult to make go away completely. I'm probably different than the standard textbook in that, but some people are always going to owe money on their credit cards, it's just something they do. But I tell them it's not an excuse: 'When the new fall clothes come out you are going to charge up a storm, I know this. We'll work on your credit card debt, but the other thing you have to have is an RRSP. You need a cushion fund.' And then we work towards that."

The Earlier You Start, the Earlier You Finish

Anne gets her employees to start saving early on in their careers, and she is doing them a favour. Starting early can make a big difference in how much you end up with. To illustrate, assume you invest one dollar each year, beginning at age 21 and stopping at age 31. Your twin sister begins investing a dollar a year at age 31 and continues to do so until age 65, earning the same interest rate as you. Assuming you are both earning at least seven percent per year on your investment until age 65, and assuming neither of you spend any of the money, your investment will be worth more than hers the entire time. This will be true at age 45, age 55, and even at age 65. Think about it: 10 years of saving early on in life beats 35 years of saving later.

Think Before You Spend

Before you buy something make sure you really want it. Before you walk over to the cash register stop for a moment. Ask yourself why you are buying. Is this something you had been planning on getting? Is this a spending priority or is it an impulse purchase that you may regret? Are you sure you'll still want it a month from now? Is it worth missing your monthly savings target for? Then, if it still seems like a good idea, make the purchase. If it does not, congratulate yourself and move on.

More Places to Free Up Extra Cash

1. **Food:** If you spend $5 per day buying lunch, then you are spending approximately $100 a month on lunch. If you could replace this with homemade lunches four out of five days each week, then you could probably save $50

per month or $600 per year.

Consider eating at home more often. Restaurant meals are often a large, hidden expense for many working women. If time is an issue, then cook one big meal each weekend and freeze four or five servings for later use. If an important reason for your restaurant meals is socializing, consider going out for coffee instead. Or order whatever you want for one course of the meal and be frugal with the other courses. For instance, order whichever entree you want, but drink tap water and skip dessert.

2. **Reading materials:** Borrow books from the library instead of buying them. Share magazines with friends. If you consistently buy a specific magazine at the checkout counter, then consider subscribing instead.
3. **Clothing:** Figure out what you like and what suits you, and try to buy classics in these styles rather than the latest fashion. It makes for a smaller clothing budget, more mix-and-match possibilities and less painful photo album sessions ten years hence. Save on dry-cleaning by washing woolens and delicate clothing by hand. Visit second-hand consignment stores.
4. **Travel:** Travel as a student. Visit friends, participate in exchanges, backpack, use hostels, get off the beaten path and only eat one meal a day in restaurants.
5. **Entertainment:** Join community interest groups and take low-cost courses. Indulge in lower-cost entertainment like coffee outings, bookstore browsing, library visits, dollar movies, book clubs, volunteering, slumber parties, board games, outdoor activities, exercise, drawing, singing and self-delivered beauty treatments. Buy used sporting and hobby equipment and stick to the basics, unless the activity involved is one of your key spending priorities. Attend free admission days at museums and galleries. Check the newspaper for free local activities.
6. **Large-ticket items:** Refinish furniture instead of buying brand new. Buy second hand. *The Bargain Finder* has great deals on appliances, office furniture, and other household items. Join a long-distance savings plan if you make a lot of long-distance calls. Consider trading services with friends or colleagues.
7. **Financial Services/Investing:** Avoid paying bank fees by getting an account in which fees are waived with a minimum balance, and maintain that minimum balance. Tax shelter your investments in your RRSP before investing in non registered savings. Shop around for the lowest-cost insurance. Consider using a discount brokerage if you plan to stick to basic mutual funds or think you know enough to invest without a broker's advice.

8. **Avoid Low-Value Added Costs:** Skip banking frills unless you absolutely need them. Don't bother with extended warranties. Have you ever actually used one? Don't lease vehicles. Cancel your cable TV if you can see the shows you want on the regular channels. Buy popular CDs through a no-commitment CD club or at a second-hand store. Don't join health clubs or start hobbies you are never going to follow through on.

Worthwhile Purchases

On the other hand, there are some things that may be worth spending more on. Credit cards that offer frequent-flyer points may make sense for you if you consistently spend over $2,000 a month on your credit card and plan to travel. Quality clothing and shoes in classic styles that will suit you over the long haul are worth more than cheaper, trendy items. Warehouse club membership may be worthwhile if you can avoid impulse shopping when you are there. Spending money on the upkeep of your car, clothes, possessions, and body means they'll last longer and require fewer repairs.

It also makes sense to hire people to do tasks for you if what you pay them is less than what you can earn in after-tax earnings during the time they free up for you. For example, it makes sense for you to pay someone to do your cleaning and lawn maintenance if this frees you up to do alternative consulting work that provides you with higher after-tax hourly income than what you pay your handy-person. Your time has value, and this value shouldn't be ignored.

Buying a Car

One of the most expensive and depreciating assets you are likely to buy is a car. Following a few basic rules can help you to reduce the cost of your transportation by thousands of dollars.

1. **Never buy a brand new vehicle:** The largest amount of depreciation on all makes and models of cars occurs in the first year. Sometimes by the time a car is a year old its resale value is as much as 30 percent less than its initial purchase price. Research the car you want, using consumer reports and library resources. When you have picked a model that fits your needs and feel confident that you are up to date on the vehicle's resale value, shop in the classified ads. Buy the car you want, but buy it used – at 12 to 24 months

old. Then spend $100 to have it inspected by a mechanic before you finalize the sale.

2. **Remember that a car is a depreciating asset, not an investment:** By the time a car is 10 years old it is usually worthless on the resale market. Think about this when you decide what kind of vehicle you want to drive. With today's escalating vehicle prices, the monthly loan payment for a high-prestige vehicle is often as much as a monthly condominium mortgage payment. Are you prepared to put this much of your hard-earned income into an asset that won't be worth anything in 10 years? Especially when you have all of these other investment options available to you?
3. **Don't be fooled by zero percent financing or reduced rate financing:** The cost of financing is factored into the total price of a vehicle, even if it isn't obviously stated. If you don't believe me, then ask a car dealer offering reduced financing how much she would be willing to reduce the price if you paid cash. She will most likely offer a reduction.
4. **Set car option priorities:** Decide which options you absolutely require as opposed to those that are simply nice to have.

Time to Spring into Action

So there you have it – 101 ideas on how to save money. I hope you've come across some new ideas that you are enthusiastic about trying. Remember that it's all about attitude. Believe that controlling your spending can be fun and rewarding, and it will be. Just as exercise milestones, like the first time you ran five miles, can make you feel like cheering, hitting savings milestone, like the first $1,000, first $10,000, first $100,000 or even first $1,000,000 in net worth, can make you feel great. So build your budget, start living it and see what you can achieve.

Making It Happen #1 – Setting a Budget

The first step to healthy money management is the right attitude. The next step is putting that attitude into action through appropriate behaviour. One of the basic tools to guide your spending behaviour is a sensible spending budget. Your budget needs to be realistic not only in terms of meeting obligations and building assets, but also in terms of emotions. In other words, do not impose spending limits that are too difficult to live with. This is the key to being able to cover your expenses and save without making the process unbearable and without inviting a binge of reactionary spending – a binge just like the eating binges are that inevitably induced by starvation dieting.

Start by recording all of your current sources of income in the budget worksheet below. Then add your basic, unavoidable expenses. These necessities generally include such things as housing expenses, utilities, local telephone service, groceries, insurance and so on.

Then fill in the list of all of the discretionary items you spend on: long-distance phone calls, cable TV, Internet access, restaurant meals, beauty treatments and so on. Note that for all of these items there are two columns in which to record figures. In the first column record how much you are actually currently spending. In the second column record an estimate of what you plan to get by on once you reduce your spending.

If you cannot get an accurate picture of your spending from past credit card statements and your chequebook, you may need to track your spending for a month or two in order to gain an accurate picture of where your money is going. Complete the second exercise below, entitled "Tracking Your Day-To-Day Expenses," and then complete your budget.

Next set a few spending priorities. Maybe yours are contributing to a vacation fund and increasing your long-distance spending in order to stay in closer touch with distant friends. Maybe they are buying a new computer and expanding your CD collection. Whatever they are, set reasonable spending targets for the next 12 months. Remain aware of what your spending priorities are, and surf for opportunities to fulfill them cost-effectively.

Finally, list the investments you plan to make in order to meet the financial goals you set in Chapter 5. Don't get concerned if you aren't completely clear on what you want to invest in. The investing section of this book will help you make specific investment decisions, and we will come back to this portion of your budget when we complete your entire personal financial plan in Chapter 17.

Monthly Income:	**$$$$$$**
Wages	
Social Assistance Payments	
Family Allowance	
Pension Income	
Annual Bonus (divided by 12)	
Other Sources of Income	
TOTAL MONTHLY INCOME:	

Expenses:

Necessities	**Current Spending**	**Revised Spending**
Mortgage Payment or Rent		
Property Tax		
Utilities:		
• Gas		
• Electricity		
• Garbage Pick-up		
• Hydro		
Phone bill:		
• Home Phone Local Service		
Professional Fees		
Food:		
• Groceries		
Insurance:		
• Car Insurance		
• Home Insurance		
• Other insurance		
Health Care Expenses Not Paid by Insurance:		
• Medical		
• Dental		
Car Operations:		
• Gas		
• Car Payments		
• Maintenance		
• Repairs		
Childcare Expenses:		
• Baby-sitting		
• School Expenses		
• Other		
Loan Payments:		
• Student Loan		
• Bank Loan		
• Credit Card Debt		
• Other		
TOTAL NECESSITIES		

Discretionary Spending	Current Spending	Revised Spending
Phone Bill:		
• Long Distance	______	______
• Cell Phone Expenses	______	______
Cable TV	______	______
Internet Access	______	______
Newspaper/Magazine Subscriptions	______	______
Food:		
• At Work Food Expenses	______	______
• Restaurant Meals	______	______
Car operations:		
• Car Washes	______	______
• Parking	______	______
Clothing	______	______
Hair Care	______	______
Beauty Treatments	______	______
Drug Store Items (personal hygiene)	______	______
Entertainment:		
• Hobbies	______	______
• Exercise	______	______
• Other Entertainment	______	______
Gifts	______	______
Donations	______	______
Travel	______	______
Pet Care Expenses	______	______
Spending Priorities		
1. ______	______	______
2. ______	______	______
3. ______	______	______
Other: ______	______	______
Other: ______	______	______
TOTAL DISCRETIONARY SPENDING	______	______
TOTAL MONTHLY EXPENSES (Total Necessities + Total Discretionary)	______	______
NET MONTHLY SAVINGS (Total Monthly Income – Total Monthly Expenses)	______	______
New Investments		
Debt Repayment	______	______
Extra Mortgage Payments	______	______
RRSP Savings	______	______
Other ______	______	______
Other ______	______	______
TOTAL NEW INVESTMENTS	______	______

Is your level of monthly savings equal to your new investments and in keeping with the financial goals you defined in Chapter 5? If not, then keep reworking your proposed budget until they are in sync. If that just doesn't seem feasible, then consider revising your financial goals or find a way to increase your income. Either way, your monthly budget, financial goals and life goals need to be in sync in order for you to succeed.

If you are unable to get to your desired net monthly savings level, then consider this idea. Next time you get a raise at work, pretend you didn't. Set up an automatic withdrawal to invest your incremental pay. If you could live off of your take-home pay the month before your raise, you can live off of it after you get your raise. Your expenses do not automatically increase when you get a raise, unless you decide to increase them. So consider taking advantage of this opportunity to increase your savings. It's relatively painless because it doesn't require any noticeable sacrifice in your day-to-day spending.

Making It Happen #2 – Tracking Your Day-To-Day Spending

If you really don't know where your money is going and you can't get a reasonable snapshot of your spending by examining your credit card statements and chequebook, then you may need to track your expenses for awhile in order to get a realistic picture. For the next month, at the end of each day, record your spending. At the end of the month, total your spending in each of the categories listed in the budget worksheet above. Then go back through the past 12 months and add in the expenditures that aren't necessarily reflected in your sample month of spending. This includes yearly expenditures such as insurance or vacations, or expenses that only occur every few months. Once you have some idea of your current spending you can set your new budget following the directions in the previous budget exercise.

In the future, if you are disciplined enough to pay off your credit card debt in full each month, I recommend that you make as many purchases as possible using one primary credit card. Making purchases by credit card or cheque will leave you with a record of most of your spending. You will be better prepared to review and reconcile your expenditures and investments with your income. Alternatively, you may wish to use one of the personal money management software packages, such as *Quicken*™, to track and categorize your spending. Either way, you'll be able to see whether you are making progress in modifying your spending habits as well as where you still need to work harder to change your habits.

8

Earning More Than Praise

It will be years – and not in my time – before a woman will lead the party or become prime minister.

Margaret Thatcher

while she was minister of health.
She became the leader of the Conservative Party the following year and prime minister in 1979.

The next four chapters move to the third stage of the prosperity equation – maximizing what you earn. Here we'll cover career selection, enhancing your advancement at work, day-to-day strategies for success on the job and the alternative of self-employment. The suggestions in this section share the wisdom of many gutsy women who, cumulatively, have hundreds of years of work experience. No matter what your current employment status or career stage, I'm sure you'll be impressed by their actions and find some useful ideas that you can utilize immediately.

Do Your Homework – It Pays

One of the first and most important career decisions you make in life concerns what to study in school. Education has a significant impact on career options and on career rewards, which, in turn, directly affect your options and your ability to ultimately achieve your life's mission. Education decisions should not be made lightly.

Within a given field it is generally true that the more education you have, the more money you can command in the marketplace. This is the case until you get to the Ph.D. level. At that point, the rewards involve further refining your knowledge and, possibly, preparing for a career in academia, but they do not involve increased earning potential.

The table below demonstrates how earnings rise with education for full-time Canadian female workers.[1]

Level of Education	1995 Average Earnings
0-8 Years of School	$20,637
Some Secondary Education	$21,971
Graduated from High School	$25,760
Some Post-secondary	$27,399
Post-secondary Certificate or Diploma	$28,840
University Degree	$42,584

The message is clear. If you can, go to school. Do your homework – it pays. Invest in your education as early in life as possible. It's the best investment you will ever make, both financially and in terms of self-development. And the earlier you do it, the longer you'll have to reap the rewards.

Even if you don't or can't earn certificates and degrees, learning in a piecemeal fashion can still pay off. If you are clear as to which career direction you want to head in, taking courses that provide you with additional skills to help you reach your goals makes sense.

Natasha, the real estate developer introduced in Chapter 5, never earned a formal degree or diploma beyond high school, but she's taken a multitude of courses that have helped her build her real estate and retailing businesses. Natasha describes her approach: "After high school I found a full-time job and studied at night. I took a mixture of business, insurance, corporate law, blueprint reading, estimating and building courses – anything that helped me learn more about real estate, since that's what I'm interested in. I took the courses wherever they were offered, whether it was a college, university or technical institute. I didn't care whether it led to a degree; what really mattered to me was that I learned what I needed to know, when I needed to know it, to further my business." Given that she owns her own successful retail business and extensive real estate holdings, Natasha's training sure seems to be paying off for her.

Even if you're not entirely clear on your career direction, taking individual courses can help you to determine what you are good at and what you enjoy doing. It can also keep you mentally challenged, strengthen your self-confidence and be a source of fun. So, if you haven't done so for a while, consider taking a course: it may well be the first step towards a more satisfying career.

Go Where the Boys Are

Katherine Whilehaen once said, "The best career advice to give the young is, find out what you like doing best and get someone to pay you for doing it." I agree. Doing something you enjoy is one of the most important criteria for choosing a profession. However, it is also important to make informed decisions regarding your career. This includes considering what you are likely to get out of the profession you enter besides personal fulfillment. After all, the majority of women work outside of the home these days, and a typical career can span 30 or 40 years. Altruistic reasons for occupational choices may earn you praise from others, but you are the one who will have to do the job day after day and who will have to live with the salary paid. Making sure you understand the starting salary and typical salary progression of the path being considered, as well as those of alternative paths that require similar skills, can help to ensure that potentially lucrative and satisfying occupations are not overlooked.

I say all of this not because money is the only thing to consider in selecting a career, but because I know that you can have money and work you enjoy at the same time. So why not do that? If you are going to spend 20 or 30 years doing something, making good money while you're at it doesn't hurt.

On average, Canadian women still earn only 73 cents for every dollar earned by a man.[2] At the same time, the higher salaries for both men and women are strongly skewed towards male-dominated professions, while low pay tends to go hand-in-hand with female-dominated professions. Personally, I always knew that the highest paying jobs were in male-dominated areas like dentistry, medicine and law, but when I reviewed salary data across all occupations in Canada, I was astonished to see how clear the link was between the percentage of men in an occupation and the average salary paid. With very few exceptions, more men equalled more money. According to 1995 census data, women held 22 percent of the jobs in the 25 top-paying occupations. Of the 25 occupations with the lowest pay, women dominate all but five.[3]

Sadly, Canadian women are still vastly over-represented in lower-paying occupations. Is it really because what women like doing best happens to be found only in these jobs? Or is it because we are in some way socialized to gravitate towards the often less-risky, lower-compensated roles? Although girls often do better than boys scholastically during primary school, we are still outnumbered in the top-paying professions. Women work in the fields that contain the top-paying jobs but usually not in the higher-paying roles. We've all been at the dentist's office with the male dentist and the female hygienist and receptionist. Likewise, do you picture a judge as male or female? How about a legal secretary? Why is it that women still tend to end up in the lower-paid support positions while men dominate the higher-paid positions?

You do not have to follow this pattern. There are many occupations that use the skills you have or are interested in developing. Make sure you understand what each of them offers and choose your direction wisely.

I'll give you an example. Assume you decided early on in life that you wanted to work in the field of health sciences. For a long time you dreamed of being a veterinarian. Then, when you began university, you decided that you wanted to work with people rather than animals. You began to think very seriously about either becoming a physiotherapist or entering medical school.

If you asked me, I would advise you to pursue medicine. It's not that I have anything against physiotherapy as a profession. But between the two options, physiotherapists earned an average of

$36,300 in 1995, whereas general practitioners and family practitioners earned an average of $97,700.[4] Both professions involve similar tasks – working with people, aiding in healing and working in the medical profession. Yet approximately 83 percent of physiotherapists were female, while only 26 percent of general practitioners were female.[5] Which one would you choose?

The whole field of medicine clearly demonstrates the male-dominated/high salary versus female-dominated/low salary rule. Occupational therapists (approximately 92 percent female) averaged $34,200. Nursing supervisors and registered nurses (approximately 95 percent female) averaged $32,700.

Even when you look at a more obscure area, like machine operators working with various substances, the female-dominate, low-paying connection is evident. Machine operators in metal and mineral product processing were approximately 5 percent female in 1995, and they earned an average of $35,100. Machine operators in fabric, fur and leather product manufacturing were 39 percent female, and they earned $17,700.

I think you get the picture. In most cases, the jobs filled mainly by men are those in which most of the money is to be found. The 20 highest-paying and lowest-paying occupations according to the 1995 census, and their corresponding share of female workers, are listed in the following tables.[6]

Jobs to Consider - 20 Highest-Paying Occupations	Percent Women	Average Full-time Workers' Salary
1. Judges	23%	$126,246
2. Specialist physicians	26%	$123,976
3. General practitioners and family practitioners	26%	$107,620*
4. Dentists	18%	$102,433
5. Senior managers in goods production, utilities, transportation and construction	8%	$99,360
6. Senior managers in finance, communications carriers and other business services	17%	$99,177
7. Lawyers and Quebec notaries	27%	$81,617
8. Senior managers in trade, broadcasting and other services	14%	$79,200
9. Primary production managers (except agriculture)	6%	$76,701
10. Securities agents, investment dealers and traders	34%	$75,911
11. Petroleum engineers	7%	$72,543
12. Chiropractors	16%	$68,808
13. Engineering, science and architecture managers	9%	$68,235
14. University professors	26%	$68,195
15. Senior managers in health, education, social and community services and membership organizations	45%	$68,187
16. Air pilots, flight engineers and flying instructors	3%	$67,581
17. Geologists, geochemists and geophysicists	11%	$66,210
18. Utilities managers	10%	$64,816
19. School principals and administrators	36%	$64,513
20. Optometrists	37%	$64,419

* Note: This income figure does not match the figure quoted earlier because figures in this table are for full-time, full-year workers only, whereas those quoted earlier are average employment income figures for all workers, including part-time workers, in each occupation.

Jobs to Avoid - 20 Lowest-Paying Occupations	Percent Women	Average Full-time Workers' Salary
1. Baby-sitters, nannies and parents' helpers	98%	$12,713
2. Food and beverage servers	76%	$14,891
3. Food service counter attendants and food preparers	75%	$15,487
4. Service station attendants	20%	$16,203
5. Harvesting labourers	54%	$16,426
6. Bartenders	55%	$16,740
7. Artisans and craftspeople	52%	$16,943
8. Ironing, pressing and finishing occupations	70%	$17,322
9. Cashiers	84%	$17,533
10. Sewing machine operators	92%	$17,613
11. Estheticians, electrologists and related occupations	96%	$17,658
12. General Farm workers	36%	$17,756
13. Tailors, dressmakers, furriers and milliners	79%	$17,850
14. Painters, sculptors and other visual artists	41%	$18,188
15. Hairstylists and barbers	75%	$18,292
16. Kitchen and food service helpers	62%	$18,799
17. Maîtres d'hotel and host/hostesses	79%	$18,873
18. Cooks	45%	$19,054
19. Hotel front desk clerks	64%	$19,220
20. Visiting homemakers, housekeepers and related occupations	90%	$19,607

As these tables make so clear, the money is generally where the men are. So, if you can, go where the men are within your chosen field and avoid the pink-collar ghettos.

Making It Happen – Getting More for Your Mastery

This exercise is designed for individuals at the planning stage in their careers, so if you are still in school, or are contemplating a career change, then this exercise is for you.

1. Name the occupation that you plan to enter ______________________

2. List the key factors that attract you to this occupation

For example, if you are planning to become a forester, then the key attractions might include the opportunity to work outside, the scientific nature of the field and a possible opportunity to help preserve nature. List your occupation's attractive features.

- ____
- ____
- ____
- ____
- ____
- ____

3. List the average starting salary for your chosen profession

$__________

(If you don't know, then go to the library or the Government of Canada website www.hrdc-drhc.gc.ca as soon as possible and find out.)

4. Write down the average overall salary in this profession

$__________

5. List at least three similar occupations

List alternative occupations that have attractive features that are similar to those in the occupation you are targeting, and their starting and average salaries.

Alternative Occupation	Starting Salary	Average Salary
• ______________	$________	$________
• ______________	$________	$________
• ______________	$________	$________

6. Are you still comfortable with your original occupation selection?

Do you want to do some more research before you commit to this option? The choice is yours.

9

Soaring Through the Turbulence

As is our confidence, so is our capacity.

WILLIAM HAZLITT

The situation Canadian women face in the work-world has changed a great deal in the past few decades. Much of the overt sexism is gone, but gender-specific hurdles and covert sexism can still be found. The challenge for us as women is to understand how the system works – a system that was originally designed by married men and in many ways still caters to their needs – and work with what we know.

While men often learn many of the unspoken rules that apply in the work-world as children, many women don't really start learning how the game is played until they begin their first full-time job. It is there that we come up against male culture and scratch our heads in puzzlement: this isn't how we were taught to play. "Why isn't everybody sharing? Why aren't people more polite?" we ask ourselves. Over time, most of us come to realize that we aren't necessarily interested in many of the rewards that are designed to motivate a stereotypical married man. We find we don't agree with a lot of the rules of the game, and we realize that there will never be a perfect fit between the corporate work-world and ourselves. But this doesn't mean that we can't adapt or even excel. Proof can be found in the lives of many of the women whose successful career strategies are offered in this chapter and the next.

Personally, it still irks me to see male workers move ahead at a disproportionate rate to their female counterparts. I wonder how much of it is a case of the best candidate being promoted, how much is due to residual sexism – old boys' clubs and subtle prejudices – and how much results from women inadvertently working against themselves.

Sexism, can be difficult to change because much of it is subtle and subconscious. It often comes into play in subjective decisions, even without the decision-maker realizing it. For instance, it is now rare for women to be told to their faces, "You aren't getting the job because you are female," as a number of my interviewees reported having happen to them 20 or 30 years ago. However, subconscious sexism may still enter hiring, pay and promotion decisions. Often these decisions are still made by men who select and reward individuals with whom they feel comfortable, and they naturally tend to feel more comfortable with other men. The actual decisions are justified through familiar rationalizations: the male contenders supposedly showed more confidence, leadership ability and so on. However, subtle, often unintentional, sexism frequently plays a role, if in no other way than in how confidence and other subjective skills are assessed. He was captain of his university football team; she chairs the committee that organizes the annual Christmas party for 1,500 employees. Who showed more leadership? The traditional answer may be the football captain. But is it really so? It's a tough call.

It's not just men who succumb to sexist influences either; all of us do it to some degree. We are programmed on a daily basis to expect, and feel more comfortable with, men in more dominant positions and females in more subordinate positions. Teachers are women and the principal is a man. Secretaries are female and the CEO is a man. That's what we are used to seeing. The challenge is to increase our consciousness of biases and to challenge ourselves and others to question our sexist beliefs. As we change the beliefs, we change the behaviour.

What's Really Going On in the Office?

In *When Work Doesn't Work Anymore*, Elizabeth Perle McKenna writes: "Being a good worker does not guarantee success. Loyalty, dedication, excellence, and hard work without some form of self-promotion or other way of being recognized often invites exile from the fast track. I have tried sitting back and hoping that someone will recognize my good work. In the culture of success this is seen as passivity – rarely an asset. Or, it's mistaken for a lack of fire, guts, or ambition."[1]

Have you experienced this situation? It's not that we are wrong to act the way we do. Good work should be rewarded and often it is. But what we sometimes don't realize is that good work, even excellent work, alone is not the ticket to success. More men understand this because they learned it while growing up.

As children, men often learn that it's not necessarily the smartest guy who leads the pack; instead, it's the guy who takes control, convinces others of his leadership and acts the part. Boys learn the importance of networking and building alliances. Even the simple things, like the way guys talk to each other and what they talk about, are things they are more familiar with than we are. Women rarely get the kind of exposure to male interaction that makes all of this second nature. So it's up to us to learn the rules of male culture and to work effectively within it.

Who's on Your Team?

In male-oriented corporate culture, whom can you trust? Should you congregate with other women or younger men? There is no hard and fast answer. There are people who will help you, and people who will harm you, and they don't belong to any one age group or sex. There are tail-end baby-boomers who will stab you in the back if it means moving themselves a notch up the corporate ladder, and there are old boys who still don't believe women belong in the boardroom. Women also can often work against each other, just as disadvantaged minorities frequently attack each other rather than the larger system that is oppressing them all. The good news, though, is that while you can't categorize the difficult people, you can learn what to watch out for.

Janine, a Toronto real estate development firm vice-president, didn't beat around the bush when I asked about the career obstacles she had faced. "My greatest fear in the workplace is incompetent, bullying men. I'm typically so focused on output, building a team and getting the job done, that I don't usually see it coming, but boy, can it get vicious. I worked for a bully for a couple of years. He caused me a lot of heartache, but, eventually, he ended up being the loser. Eventually he shot himself in the foot.

"Still, I found it very, very difficult and ended up seeking professional advice on how to handle it. I went to a doctor who basically empowered me to deal with the bully. It was very helpful because I think that women of my generation are not well trained on how to handle intimidating men."

Janine's story is not atypical for women of any generation. Many women, when faced with a situation like this, feel ill prepared and powerless. Luckily for Janine, she was strong enough to seek outside advice and encouragement in order to defend herself rather than turning and running.

We are all bound to encounter a bully at work sometime, and dealing with this situation successfully usually requires us to stand up for ourselves and to set clear boundaries as to the behaviour we will and will not tolerate from others. Amazingly, once they are confronted and boundaries are clearly communicated, many bullies back off and look for a more complacent target.

It may be difficult to believe you have power, and it may be scary to claim that power and use it to protect yourself, but you can do it. It will not destroy you, as you may subconsciously think. It will not make people think less of you. In fact, it usually ends up helping you see that most people don't want bullies to be tolerated any more than you do and that many people are ready and willing to help if you let them. And, realizing that you have rights and don't need to accept abusive behaviour in the workplace or anywhere else, will make you stronger. It is hard to do, but once you do it for the first time, you're far less likely to be intimidated again.

Who's on the Opposing Team?

Colette, a veteran of the communications industries, shares her experience of moving up the corporate ladder. "Probably some of the worst work experiences I've had in my life have been with women. Don't make the assumption that because someone is a woman they are actually going to be supportive and nurturing. It's not necessarily the case because the institutions don't support that kind of behaviour."

Colette makes a good point. While Janine had her worst work experience with a male bully, it doesn't mean that female colleagues are necessarily going to be your strongest allies. Unfortunately, most corporations still reward aggressive male-culture behaviour, regardless of whether it is exhibited by a woman or a man. So it's not surprising that sometimes women undermine each other.

Colette continues, "As you start moving into more senior levels, it starts to get really ugly. You find out that a lot of women have moved higher by acting like men, and they exhibit many of the same behaviours. One of the greatest disappointments is when you discover that women often don't support other women and that you might be more likely to find your support from the men sitting around the table. It's quite a shocking, interesting discovery.

"Then you've got the old boys, who in many cases aren't even aware that they are being sexist. It's just what was acceptable their whole life. Now many of them have daughters who are lawyers and doctors and they want their daughters to do really well, so they may even be re-evaluating some of their behaviour. In my mind, they are not necessarily particularly damaging.

"Then you've got the young boy. You always thought that these guys who grew up with us and were our peers were going to have these great work relationships with us and everything was going to work out well. My experience is that they can actually be the most mean-spirited and competitive of the lot if it contributes to their success.

"So you thought you were going to get support from the women in the senior jobs and you thought you were going to get your support from this new generation of men, and what a terrible disappointment to discover that it's not going to come from either place. In fact, you find that your best support is from that old guy you thought was the dinosaur who needed to kick-off!"

Colette's analysis may sound negative, but I think it's realistic. The higher you go, the more competitive it is likely to be simply because the people who get there tend to be more competitive than the average person. This can be difficult for women to deal with because we often aren't well prepared to deal with the "male brand" of competitiveness; instead, we grew up with a female culture that promoted co-operation and politeness in good times and back-stabbing in bad. These tactics don't always work terribly well within male culture.

WHAT ABOUT HER?

One of the big mistakes some women make is buying into and feeding the office gossip put-downs of other women in the workplace. Let's look at a specific example. Lisa describes what she experienced within the academic environment as a nursing instructor.

"The university president and his assistant were really patronizing towards the nurses. They sent clear messages that they thought we couldn't get along together and that was really the root of any problem we might have. I heard that many times. It's that old business of saying that the reason that women get into trouble or that women don't get ahead is because they fight and don't get along.

"I think it still goes on today. Women buy into it too and don't stop to analyze why it happens. I think it has a lot to do with not having power. When you don't have power and you can't act out against the people who do have power, you sometimes take it out within your own group.

"Men don't see it that way, and women often adopt the male conclusion that it's really women who can't get along, but that actually has never been my experience. I've always pursued work with women and I can honestly say that I've had very good working relationships with women over many years."

Can you think of any examples of this in your own work-life? I remember once working within a close team of five women and finding that we all needlessly undermined each other. The real problem was that our team was seriously understaffed and that, given the resources with which we had been provided, there was no way we could accomplish the tasks with which we had been charged. Yet instead of presenting a united front and arguing for adequate resources, we took it out on each other. The rest of the department complacently accepted our misanalysis and mishandling of the situation. What a shame that we spent a year fighting amongst ourselves instead of banding together and demanding fair treatment from the organization.

Work with Allies

The lesson in all of this is to look for, and work with, allies. The more the better; you can never have too many people on your side. So rather than putting your head down and focusing just on doing the job at hand as best you can, make time to get to know the people around you. Build relationships and make confidantes. Maybe that means making a point of asking a different colleague to coffee or lunch once a week. Or speaking to the people you pass in the hall. Or joining the office running team. Decide what feels most comfortable for you and do it. It's like buying an insurance policy for your future. And make sure you include some female colleagues in your ally ranks. When times are tough, it can be especially helpful and comforting to have female friends who can relate to what you're going through and offer advice.

In every organization and in every work experience there are people who want to help you succeed. These are people who want to help others as they themselves have been helped and/or who simply want their workplace to be a more humane environment. You just need to open yourself to their presence and you will see them everywhere. Believe they are there and you will see them. In fact, the more you believe they are there, and the more you believe you have the power and the right to work with positive individuals, the more you will experience them in your life and the less you will notice the negative individuals around you. You'll gravitate towards those who are positive and move away from those who are negative.

Look for Mentors

Dale, the owner of a market research firm, spoke of how an older female colleague helped her start her own business and how they developed a strong friendship along the way. "While I was doing my masters degree I was working for an older woman named Jill. She was much older, actually a mother of a friend of mine. She had been an at-home market researcher for 20 years when I met her. She really was very typical of the industry at that point. She worked out of her house and had a group of 15 or 20 women who worked for her out of their own homes. The market research companies would call her up and say. 'We have work to do in Edmonton, can you make the calls?' She would take the work and divide it up among all of the women who worked for her.

"I worked with her on and off until she was 75 years old. Then I started to take over the business from her. She would need help and I would take on a project. Over time, Jill, who was a wonderful soul, gave me all of her contacts. I started out with one major client of my own and all of Jill's previous clients – about a dozen in total – a small office and short-term rent. And that's where it began. Then I realized that I enjoyed it, and I've been in business 12 years."

And so it goes. For every difficult person there are 10 others who are easy to work with, so don't get scared off by the bullies. There are always bumps in the road; there are always difficult people to deal with. Be on the lookout for troublemakers, use the resources you have and take advantage of other people's offers of support and help. Cultivate informal mentors. Ask for a formal mentor. Remember that each of us has the personal power to stand up for what we believe is right, and each of us has the ability to choose to exercise our power as we see fit. Exercise your power and your choice when you get pushed further than you are willing to accept.

Take Control of Your Career Because No One's Going to Do It for You

If you don't think of what you do for a living as a career, then start. Whether you spend 3 hours a day or 12 hours a day working, whether you plan to spend 3 years at it or 30 years at it and whether you get paid $6 an hour or $60 an hour for it what you choose to spend your adult wage-earning years doing is your career. As such, it should be taken seriously. How else are you going to get what you deserve out of it?

Whether you are male or female, taking ownership of your own career is important. You should know what you like to do, where you want to go and what your long-term goals are. The same as with your financial health – if you aren't able to visualize where you'd like to end up career-wise, then you're very unlikely to get there. This doesn't mean that you need to know the exact title of the job you want to have 20 years from now; rather, you need to be clear on the general direction you want to take so that you can successfully surf for career opportunities. Your career goals also need to be in sync with your life goals. How did you define your life goals in Chapter 2? Are your career goals in sync with them? And are both consistent with your financial goals? Or do you need to make adjustments in one or more of these areas?

Your career goals may be focused on the type of work you want to be doing or the types of skills you want to be using. They may be linked to the level of power or authority you wish to achieve. They may be linked to the type of working environment in which you wish to find yourself. They can be defined however you want, just as long as they are meaningful to you. For my part, I express my long-term career goals as:

1. **To be doing work that I am proud of and that enables me to express my creativity.**
2. **To earn an excellent income doing what satisfies me.**

For me, this is as specific as I want to get. And with these two long-term objectives in view, I constantly surf my mind and my environment for the career moves that will bring me closer to all of the important elements contained in these two statements. For instance, work I am proud of may involve building my own business, writing this book or increasing sales and profits in a consumer product conglomerate. I would be proud of all of these activities and would consider them a worthwhile use of my time. At the same time, knowing I want to focus on work I am proud of means, among other things, that I wouldn't want to work for a cigarette manufacturer.

The phrase "express my creativity" refers to the fact that I know I want a creative component to my work. For me, creativity can range from creating actual artwork to thinking creatively about how to run my business. Many kinds of creativity energize me, and I am somewhat flexible as to where they may emerge. I also know that a highly analytical or detail-oriented role, with little room to "think outside of the box," would drag me down. The point is to figure out what the crucial elements are for you and then allow them to guide your decisions.

You are the only person who can figure this out; no one can do it for you. If you don't know what you want to do and where you want to end up, then start thinking about it now. If you don't know what you are aiming for, then it is very hard to recognize the options in front of you and even harder to decide which path to follow. Here are some potential ways to gather more information to help you further clarify your short-term and long-term career goals:

- Read a career-planning book like *What Color Is Your Parachute?* by Richard Nelson Bolles.
- Attend a career-planning workshop.
- Ask other people about their work to determine whether or not you might be interested in it.
- Ask someone who is working in a field you are interested in if you can observe her at work for a day.
- Talk to your co-workers, people in related industries with whom you come into contact and your manager about what they think your options are.
- Conduct information-gathering interviews with people in fields you think might be of interest to you.
- Look through your school's alumni records to find alumni who might be willing to provide you with information.
- Ask friends and relatives if they know of anyone relevant to whom they could introduce you.
- Go to the library or on-line and research your career options.

I have done most of these things at various points in my career. With regard to all of the networking suggestions, it has been rare that anyone has ever denied me a meeting. Most people who enjoy what they do love to talk about their jobs. Furthermore, many people who manage others are always on the lookout for a good potential candidate and, therefore, are interested in meeting with people who are interested in their field.

Make Sure You Know Where You're Headed

All of this should provide you with a mental roadmap of where you plan on heading. The roadmap may have many potential paths in it, it may be kind of vague and faded or you may be one of those rare and lucky people who know exactly where you are going and the most direct path to get there. My own map has paths to numerous potential areas in the fields of business and art. Most of the potential paths on my map pull the two fields together in some way. Road signs labeled film production and consumer product marketing, as well as my own business, all involve some degree of overlap between creativity and business: that is why they are on my map. I have some idea of what is achievable in each of these career options, what the trade-offs and lifestyle would be and what my likelihood of success would be. I don't know yet which of these paths I will ultimately follow – most likely I will follow each of them at different times in my life – but what I do know is the general direction in which I am heading.

Your map will give you a framework within which to make decisions about which way to go, which opportunities to pursue, which to drop and where to focus your energy on a day-to-day basis. Without a map you fall into the danger of wandering aimlessly.

Taking ownership of your career also means proactively moving it along the path. This means working towards acquiring needed skills, asking for opportunities and rewards along the way and making sure you let people around you know your long-term goals. Keep your vision for your future on your own radar screen and make sure that it is clear to the people around you. You'll be surprised at how "picturing it in your head" and "projecting it out there" work together to keep moving you closer to your goals.

Keep Your Eye on the Prize

Having a career plan also means that you need to keep your eye on the prize. Where do you ultimately want to end up? That is the prize. All the positive steps along the way, those are the treats you've earned. Don't feel embarrassed for going after it and don't feel greedy. In the corporate world it is highly unlikely that you'll ever be given more than you've earned and deserve.

Janine says we should accept the rewards that come our way and avoid the tendency to be honest to a fault when we express our career plans at work. "Note the career paths available and pursue one or more of them. Period. End of story. Women are not good at that. You have to focus both on what you are doing right now and looking ahead. You have to do both. For example, if you decide that you are only going to be with a company for five years, keep that to yourself and go for all of the promotions possible because you could always change your mind. All of a sudden you may decide you want to stay and you may have missed two or three good opportunities if you are too honest about your plans. It's very important to move up wherever you are."

Don't sabotage yourself by worrying that you're not ready for the opportunity that is offered to you. It was offered to you because you are more ready than anyone else available for the job. Feel free to go for it.

Don't think that the lack of positive feedback means you are not doing good work. The men around you just weren't brought up expecting to give or receive the continual feedback that most women crave. A lack of positive feedback doesn't mean people think you are not doing a good job, negative feedback does. Until you get negative feedback assume you are doing well and make sure you get rewarded for your hard work.

Believe in Yourself

It all comes down to how you feel about yourself. Self-confidence is an important factor in determining what you can achieve in life and in your career. Yet we are usually our own worst critics, and we often judge ourselves more harshly than men judge themselves.

So how do you build your self-esteem, come to believe you deserve more and go after it? Jane's story tells how she met the challenge of adequately valuing her own skills and, in the process, built a thriving and lucrative consulting practice.

Jane's transition from poorly paid academic to high-priced consultant began with the encouragement of friends. "A good friend was having a dinner party and invited me. At the party a male guest was complaining that his firm had implemented five organizational change processes but didn't know how to measure whether or not they had had any impact. Since this was an area I knew about, I said, 'Well I can show you how to do that!' He was intrigued and asked me for a written proposal. I immediately froze and said, 'I can't, I don't know how to write a proposal.' Luckily some of the other consultants at the party jumped in and offered to help me with it, and we wrote the proposal shortly thereafter.

"Next I got called for an interview with the company. I panicked. I had nothing suitable to wear. I called my woman friends. One lent me a briefcase, somebody else gave me a coat, and somebody offered me a suit. I was outfitted by an entire team of women and, in the end, it was really useful because it gave me confidence during the interview. I felt like I was a composite of all of the women whose clothes I was wearing. So when I was answering the questions it was Susan who was answering, or Leslie or any of them, but not me, and it was really easy. I got the job!

"Then when I first started consulting I went through a phase where I thought, 'I can't believe they are paying me all of this money for this!' I was suffering from the impostor syndrome. It reminded me of when I defended my dissertation and thought, 'I know this is not good. They know this is not good. Somebody is going to find out. If I just squeeze through I'll never do anything so bad again.' Then when I realized that people were willing to pay me for my knowledge, it was quite a revelation.

"It took a number of years to gain my confidence as a consultant. When I started consulting in 1980, I would stand in front of a group of clients, but I would stand behind a chair, behind a table, against the wall. And then one of my clients helped me come out from behind the chair and out from behind the table. I wanted to scuttle back and hide behind the chair and the table again. And then I thought, 'These people are not stupid. If they think I can provide value then maybe I am providing value.' I began to notice that some of the things I did made a difference, and I thought, 'Okay, I am having an impact.'

"Over the years, as I continued to consult, I realized that I was actually working a lot harder than other consultants who were earning a lot more money than I was. And I thought, 'Am I being a silent partner in this?' I thought, 'I've got to take charge of my own destiny here. I have spent all of these years on my education, I have all of these experiences and I seem to know more than a lot of other people do.' So I started feeling much less guilty about what I made and a lot more confident asking for what I am worth."

Jane's early career paints a classic picture of how, as women, we often tend to undervalue ourselves in the work-world. Throughout our lives the message is reinforced that we are worth less than our male counterparts. We see men portrayed in high-paid leadership positions in movies and on TV, and, for many of us, our fathers were the family breadwinners.

However, like Jane, you too can undertake the gradual process of increasing your belief in yourself and your value. Once you believe in your worth you are much more likely to ask for and receive the compensation you deserve. Jane now confidently charges up to $1,000 per day for her services, and she is constantly in demand. She knows she is worth it, and so do her clients. In the end, people believe about you what you believe about yourself.

Making It Happen: Creating a Praise List

As females, we are often taught early on to measure our self confidence by outside praise. In school we respond well to feedback and, generally, earn higher marks than do boys. We are taught to praise each other. As working adults, we rarely get the steady stream of feedback we are conditioned to expect, and, as a result, our confidence can suffer. If you've experienced this, then creating a praise list will help.

In the back of your journal or in a file folder at work, keep track of every positive piece of feedback you get on the job. Regardless of whether it comes from your boss, your peers, a customer or anyone else, write it down. Date each entry. Then, when your confidence level is low, turn to your list and read.

We can take criticism very personally, even though its genesis may have been someone else's bad day, jealousy or insecurity. By counterbalancing the negative with the positive we can stay confident and stay in the game.

10

Claiming Your Just Desserts

Diamonds are only chunks of coal,
That stuck to their jobs, you see.

MINNIE RICHARD SMITH

Corporate Canada may still favour men, but things are changing as more and more of us assert ourselves, ask for what we deserve and gain increasing power and influence. This chapter is dedicated to helping you ensure you receive all of the rewards you deserve for your work.

YOU'VE GOT THE POWER

Almost every job has a range of pay tied to it. Your actions can make the difference between whether you are paid at the bottom of your job's pay scale or at the top. In the movie *Thelma and Louise*, Louise comments, "You get what you settle for." This couldn't be truer in the work-world. Don't, like many women, settle for less than you are worth. You may think there really isn't much room for adjustment, but the mere fact that we, as women, on average, still earn less than our male counterparts in the same jobs indicates that there is plenty of room to manoeuvre.

This is true even at the highest levels of business. A 1997 survey by Catalyst, a New York women's research group, found that women managers in the private sector earn 58 cents for every dollar earned by white male managers. In 1996, the five highest-paid female CEOs' median total compensation, excluding stock options and miscellaneous pay, was $981,192.[1] That was 48 percent less than the $1.9 million median income for CEOs at the 500 largest publicly traded U.S. companies, according to Executive Compensation Advisory Services. Tara Parker-Pope of *The Wall Street Journal* suggests that one reason for this is that women may be less likely then men to have peers with whom to compare notes. Mary Mattis, vice-president of research and advisor services at Catalyst, says, "Men talk about this stuff on the golf course and in the bars and among themselves all of the time." Do you compare notes with your colleagues?

What else can you do to make sure you are getting a fair deal? Let's explore some of the day-to-day strategies and tactics that have been used successfully by many women to build their incomes.

What Are You Worth Today?

In order to make sure you are rewarded properly for your contribution, you must know your own value. You should, at all times, have a good idea of what the market is paying for people with your qualifications. I know numerous people who routinely go on interviews to test the market. In fact, it is often people who work in the field of human resources who do this. If a co-worker happens to find out that they attended an outside interview, then they simply explain that they have always stayed in touch with the marketplace and were simply checking market conditions. They don't announce they are doing this, but they also don't avoid interviews or conversations with headhunters.

Another way of calculating your worth to your employer is to think about your replacement value. What would it cost your company to fill your position if you were to leave? Would they have to pay for an expensive recruiting process? Would they have to hire a headhunter? How much would it cost them to train someone? These are all factors to take into consideration in estimating your replacement value.

Knowing both your market value and your replacement value is useful. These figures help you to determine whether or not you are being fairly compensated. Knowing the facts may also motivate you to ask for a raise if you think that your compensation is too low, and they can be very useful when building your case for more money.

Requests, Not Demands

At one point in my own career I moved from marketing to a new cross-training assignment in sales. Because no one else in the company filled the same role, I couldn't directly compare my salary to anyone else's. However, during the first few months on the job, I was privy to a fair amount of information about the individual compensation of various sales force members, and I concluded that I was being significantly underpaid. I knew it wasn't going to be easy to convince my manager that I deserved more money. He had a reputation for being a tough salary negotiator, and it was six months away from our annual compensation review date. However, I was determined to get a raise. So I booked a meeting with him.

I brought notes to the meeting, detailing the facts that I thought supported my case. First, I outlined the increased level of responsibility that came with my new role. Then I listed all of the specific relevant salary figures I could find to prove that I wasn't being adequately compensated. I included the average starting salaries of the latest graduating class of students from my MBA program. I cited salaries I knew were being offered by a couple of competitive firms for people in my position. I also compared my total compensation to that of my sales colleagues with the same level of experience, taking into account the value of their year-end bonuses and company cars – two valuable perks I didn't get. I stated my case verbally, covering each item I had written down as calmly as possible, and asked for a raise. My manager asked a few clarifying questions and then said he would think about it. I decided to let it rest for the time being and waited. Luckily, I didn't need to re-broach the subject. A few weeks later I was given a raise.

In retrospect, I think I did a lot of things right. Based on research from a number of different information sources, I knew that my pay was not comparable to others with similar backgrounds, experience and responsibilities. I was organized and tactful in my presentation. I didn't make it personal; I stuck to the facts. I stayed as unemotional and as objective as possible. And I proceeded one step at a time, giving my boss a chance to consider what I had to say and to act on it before I brought it up again. I think the thing that most convinced him to give me a raise was the salary information I provided from competitive companies. You see, I didn't say how I got it. I let him assume that I got the information through headhunters approaching me with other job opportunities when, in fact, it came from friends who had considered the jobs. I let him think I might leave if I didn't get more pay, but it wasn't presented as a threat – it was merely an implied suggestion. Sometimes what you don't say is more valuable than what you do say.

Possibly there really is no room for salary movement in your job. Is there something else you want and think you deserve? How about working from home part-time, more vacation time, a training course or a new office chair? How are people in your position at other companies being rewarded? Whether in the form of money or something else, now is the time to research your value, develop your argument, make a request and see what happens. You'll never know unless you ask.

Keep in mind that one of the most potentially valuable rewards is equity. Company shares, stock options, share of revenue, royalties and content ownership are all potential ways to own a piece of the business and its upside potential. If it is feasible in your field, then be on the lookout for these types of rewards and go after them.

Let's look at another example of a woman asking directly for something she thinks she deserves.

Silence Isn't Always Golden

Jennifer is a 34-year-old new business development manager for a bank. Before moving to her current role she was an account manager for the same organization. During that time, a job opening became available for a regional manager and Jennifer applied. The job was given to a married male colleague who had less management experience and was performing far below Jennifer in terms of meeting his sales quota. Furthermore, Jennifer had already demonstrated her ability to do the job in question by handling it for a four-month period while the previous regional manager was absent. Jennifer was convinced that the decision to give the job to her male colleague was unfair.

Instead of feeling angry but saying nothing, Jennifer talked to her manager about his hiring decision and shared her bottom line. Jennifer knew what type of person her manager was, and she knew she could be very honest and direct with him. As a result, she not only explained that she thought he had made a bad decision, but also told him that she was frustrated to the point of considering leaving.

In the end, Jennifer was offered a newly created position entitled New Business Development Manager, more responsibility and an $8,000 raise. She doubts she would have been offered the job if she hadn't addressed the issue directly.

Interestingly, when Jennifer's boss made her the offer, Jennifer responded by saying that she would need a few days to think about whether the new position, with its alternative role and additional responsibility, was something she wanted to take on. After thinking it over she accepted the position.

What did Jennifer do right? She let her boss know how she felt about not getting the original job. She was clear about her career expectations and was able to express them honestly. She skipped the old, "Say nothing, bury the anger and either take it out on the company in other ways or leave in frustration routine." This is wise because, ultimately, taking it out on the company in other ways, usually by performing your job below your potential, just ends up hurting you. It gives the firm a reason to overlook you again when the next promotion comes up. The alternative of leaving is not very good either. Ultimately, you can only change jobs so many times and still keep your resume looking respectable. Save those moves for the really big things, like a solid move upward, escaping a dead-end job or a glass ceiling, or accommodating personal life priorities. Assertive honesty will serve you much better than passive aggressiveness.

Jennifer didn't appear desperate. When she asked for time to think the alternative job over, she wasn't playing games; she really wanted to think it over. Once she was clear that she did want to accept the position offered, she told her boss immediately. Through the process she let her manager sweat a little, but she was really doing it to take the time she needed and deserved to make sure she was making a good decision. Taking time to make decisions, rather than feeling like you should accept immediately in humble gratitude, is your right; and you deserve to exercise it.

Jennifer was open and honest, she stood up for herself and it paid off. If you are good at what you do and you deserve something you aren't getting, share your expectations with your boss. The worst you can hear is "No." Even that is valuable. It gives you valuable information about where you stand in your current job. This is information that will help you decide whether you want to stay where you are or not. Not asking and not finding out where you stand leaves you with little objective information with which to work.

Jennifer's advice to other women: "I think you've got to be honest with people. I've too often seen women sit back and say, 'Oh, I didn't get it.' I think you've got to be honest with your boss and say, 'I deserved the promotion, I know I did.' You have to be able to provide them with reasons why it is unfair and you have to justify why you feel that way, but I think you have to let them know. If you don't ask, they are not going to give it to you. If you think you need a raise, you have to ask for it. If you want a promotion, you have to ask for it. Polite doesn't work and bosses aren't fair."

Jennifer makes some very good points. Be direct. Know your worth. Promote your worth. Female socialization may make you feel uncomfortable with being direct and stating your expectations. These actions may seem greedy and selfish to you. However, if you do it in the right instances (when it really matters to you) and in the right way (with an objective, fact-based, unemotional rationale), then you are likely to be perceived by those around you as possessing self-confidence and you are likely to be respected for it.

Sit in Every Seat

The best negotiating strategy I know of is to examine the issue at hand from all parties' perspectives before starting to negotiate. If you know what each party wants out of the situation, you are much more likely to find a solution that is mutually agreeable. If you have figured out where your counterpart is coming from before you sit down to talk, you are more likely to come up with a solution that you like and that he is likely to accept. Knowing how to do this, and practising good negotiating techniques, is something that will serve you well in many facets of your life.

Let's go back to the example of asking for a raise. Before you ask for one, think about what your boss wants. Probably he doesn't want to have to find someone else to do your job. Probably he has a problem giving you a raise because if other people find out, and they always do, then they will want one too. So maybe what would work for you is an alternative form of increased compensation – payment for a course you want to take, some extra vacation time, a computer to allow you to work from home. If you think about your bottom line and his before you sit down, then you are more likely to come away with a win-win solution.

Facts, Not Feelings

Debra's story demonstrates how she, a 31-year-old marketing manager, is learning to be more direct in her on-the-job communication. Debra is determined to take things less personally and to focus on resolving issues that arise in a direct, objective manner, focusing on facts and behaviour rather than on personalities and emotions. By doing this she is able to resolve sensitive issues instead of dwelling on them or internalizing them as self-criticism.

"Over the course of my career I've learned technical skills, and my biggest challenge now is learning how to work through others more effectively. A big part of this is communication."

Debra explains her perspective on male-female workplace communication: "I think what happens is that women generally have a tendency to express things more than men. It seems to me, that when something is bothering us, we can't just let it go. We need to find a way of expressing it, rather than second-guessing whether we should or shouldn't say something. Men seem to find it easier to walk in and say something that they mean to toss at us like a rock, but that hits us like a boulder. We are left thinking, 'What did I do to deserve that?' We take the blame for it and we try to make up for it.

"I am learning how to stop myself from doing that; instead, I try to think, 'What just happened here?' Maybe I need to go address it with the person. Nine times out of ten, in the past, I would have thought, 'Oh well, I'll have to try to make it up some other time,' or 'He's not right and he's a jerk.' Well, I'm a jerk if I don't go and say, 'You know, I've got to tell you I didn't really feel right about what just happened' and deal with the issue directly.

"For example, a couple of weeks ago I had an uncomfortable experience at work. I was meeting with my boss and our sales managers and I was trying to convince the sales managers to use their discretionary funding for a marketing program I was proposing. I finally got them to agree, but it was like pulling teeth.

"Frustrated, I talked to my boss about it and asked for some feedback. He gave me some and then asked, 'Did I support you well enough in the meeting when you asked for the money?' Initially I responded, 'Yeah, I knew what you were thinking.' But after I thought about it, I went back to his office and said, 'I've got to be honest with you, I didn't think you gave me any support at all.' He responded with, 'You told me you knew that I was supporting your request.' And I said, 'I knew you agreed with my request because we had talked about it before the meeting, but the sales managers had no idea where you stood and you didn't say anything. To me, supporting me is saying you are aligned with my decision in front of other people.'

"In the end I felt better about the whole thing because I stood up for what I needed to stand up for. Women often take things personally and we tend to want harmony, so we often don't speak our minds. We know that it is hard and someone might not like us for it. We know we may not achieve anything from it. Look around at women in high positions, there is a very fine line between being considered good and being considered a bitch. But I find, for myself, that it is liberating when I do confront these issues, and I think, in the end, people respect you for it."

Debra provides an excellent example of a woman speaking up and being honest about someone else's behaviour – her boss's – that was not what it should have been. She expressed herself well, using "I" statements to take ownership of her perceptions. She focused on specific behaviour rather than judging or labeling her boss's actions in a way he might take personally and feel affronted by. She also described the behaviour she would have rather seen from him, leaving him with a solution for future interactions. Best of all, instead of internalizing the entire situation, taking personal responsibility for it and feeling bad about it, she dealt with it directly. She didn't allow it to become a negative subconscious thought, waiting to take its toll on future interactions among everyone involved. And, last of all, it was an isolated, non-critical incident for her to address as practice for larger, more critical issues that are likely to arise at some point in her career.

Show Us What You Can Do

Hand in hand with asking for what you are worth is making sure your contributions to the company are visible. In particular, if you want to move up the corporate ladder, then you generally first need to prove that you can do the next job. Doing your current job really well is important, but moving up usually requires you to demonstrate that you have the skills or qualities desired for the next level. This entails being on the lookout for opportunities to demonstrate these skills – whether it's stepping into a more senior role to cover for someone temporarily absent or working on a special project that allows you to demonstrate skills you don't normally use in your current role. It's up to you to figure out what the critical skills are in the role you next want to have and to find ways to develop and demonstrate those skills. Then make sure the individuals responsible for promoting you know you are interested and see the work you are doing.

Take Calculated Risks

Nadine, a senior banking official with over 20 years of experience in the financial services industry, echoes this advice to the younger women around her. Here's what she tells the women she mentors: "I encourage them to take risks. And to get out of staff jobs and into line jobs where results can be measured and where they will be rewarded. The women I know who have taken the risks have been well rewarded.

"In my own career, at one point I was asked to take a promotion into the technology area of the business. I have to tell you, I remember sitting down and doing a list – the pluses and minuses of managing this new technology department – not the least of which was that I was technologically illiterate. Even though there were pluses, my comfort level was much higher with staying where I was. At the same time I thought, 'Well if I don't take the risk I will never know.' If you fail, there is always a chance to regroup. Nothing is the end of the world.

"Now, I'm not talking about a hold-your-nose-and-jump-off-the-cliff risk. There needs to be a balance between the risk, the reward and your comfort level. But I think that women need to push themselves beyond their comfort level a little bit, both in terms of a career point of view and from a financial planning and an investing point of view.

"I think the reason women don't take on risk is this fear of ending up a bag lady. I've sat in on seminars with extremely wealthy women (for example, women whose family names are the names of brand products), and even they have this fear of becoming a bag lady. I am amazed at how prevalent that theme is across all social classes and economic classes! I think a lot of it may stem from women's historic dependence on the male members of their family for their security. In fact, I've seen research that shows that women equate money with security, whereas men equate it more with success."

So often women short-change themselves when it comes to taking on new responsibilities and roles at work. Nadine believes this stems from a deep-seated fear of not being able to take care of ourselves and, hence, the fear of jeopardizing our security in life. I think it also comes from confidence-killing childhood messages like: "Be modest. Don't brag. Make sure everybody likes you. Be careful."

Know and believe that you can take promotions and risks, that you can even fail once in awhile, and that you will still be a good and valuable employee. Step up to bat when the chance is offered; most likely you'll hit the ball a lot harder and a lot higher than you'd ever give yourself credit for.

Make Yourself Known

Having the next opportunity handed to you is nice, but it's usually the exception. The reality is that you usually need to go after it. Inez explains how she has surfed for opportunities during her career: "I have to say that most of the time I've just taken the opportunities that were there. I have always liked challenges and learning new things. So I always tried to put myself in a place that prepared me for new opportunities.

"One thing I think people don't do enough is make themselves known. I made a point of making sure my name gets known, even if it's a trivial thing, like making sure that if I wrote a report my name was on it. Other people say, 'Well, it doesn't really matter,' but it does matter. People have to know your name, otherwise how are they going to think about you when an opportunity comes up?"

Inez always knew she wanted to move up, and she took opportunities even if they weren't exactly on the path she thought she wanted to travel because she intuitively knew that, over time, they would bring her closer to her goals. This meant occasional stints performing tasks that weren't her favourites because she thought that this would be valuable in the long run.

Be Brave Socially – Build Contacts

Inez continues: "I also used to go to oodles of retirement parties early on in my career. At the time there was a whole wave of men who joined my organization after the Second World War, and they were all retiring. So I'd go to any retirement party if I knew the retiree to any degree. Again, how's anybody going to know to give you an opportunity if they don't know you exist? So rather than dreaming about what I wanted to do with my career, I mingled and made myself known.

"The retirement parties were a good venue because they weren't by-invitation-only kind of events. You pay your $20 and go. I mean, I felt nervous introducing myself to people I didn't know. Actually I still do. But I just do it. Nobody is going to say, 'Well what are you doing here?' or any of those things that you imagine. It feels like they are, but you wouldn't say that to a friend and nobody's going to say it to you either. Everybody has a certain amount of social politeness that you can rely on."

Inez's retirement party strategy really impresses me. Everyone groans when you mention networking, but Inez found a very unique and effective way to do this for herself.

Networking sometimes gets a bad name because people confuse it with sucking-up or feigning interest in others. It doesn't have to be awkward. Networking really is just getting to know other people and finding out that you have common ground. Then when either of you comes across a piece of information that the other might appreciate, or a contact that might be useful, you share it. The more people who know what your ambitions are, the more likely it is that someone will be able to help you reach your goals. A recent survey of 22- to 24-year-olds reported that over one-third of them found work through friends or relatives rather than through formal job-hunting techniques.[2] Who you know is absolutely vital to opening up opportunities for yourself.

Companies are not benevolent associations. You are in the driver's seat when it comes to your career. Think about where you are headed. Revisit your progress along the way, figure out what you need to get there and market yourself. Be brave, be open to new ideas and experiences and to the help of others, and you'll be well on your way. Do what feels right for you. Don't wait around for someone else to do it for you.

Making It Happen – Reverse Role-playing

If you are feeling nervous about approaching others in order to address important issues, then you might want to try some reverse role-playing first. To do this, first find a willing volunteer whose career savvy you admire. Explain the issue you want to address and what you plan to say. Then role-play the meeting with your coach, but reverse your roles. You play the person you plan to confront while your friend plays you. This way you will be able to hear what your arguments sound like from the receiving end, and you can verbalize the responses you think you may get. You will see how your volunteer, who is not personally enmeshed in the situation, handles the objections. If some of the objections stump them, then the two of you can brainstorm responses once the role-playing is finished.

This practice will increase your confidence about handling the situation, show you what it's like to receive the message you plan to send and give you the opportunity to refine your planned communication.

11

Queen Of The Castle

I always wanted to be somebody. If I made it, it's half because I was game enough to take a lot of punishment along the way and half because there were a lot of people who cared enough to help me.

ALTHEA GIBSON

One of the fastest-growing work options for Canadian women is self-employment. Today, women lead over 30 percent of Canadian firms.[1] Moreover, over the last five years, the number of self-employed women in Canada grew at twice the rate as did the number of self-employed men.[2] And women's horizons are broadening. Rather than in the traditional female-owned retail venture, the number of self-employed women is now growing most rapidly in the less traditional industry sectors of finance, insurance, real estate, transportation and communications as well as in the services sector.[3]

Trust Your Gut and Just Keep Going

Judy is a great example of a woman who has entered an unconventional business arena; she is a pioneer in the ostrich business. Judy first became interested in ostriches in the late 1980s when she and her husband became ostrich producers. After a rocky start, near bankruptcy and a divorce, Judy decided to start a new business on her own, focusing on the industry from a different angle. Rather than focusing on raising the birds herself, Judy decided to work on developing the market for live ostriches, ostrich meat and other ostrich products around the world. In May 1993 she started Agribird Marketing and Sales.

Judy describes how she began to build her business. "I went out and talked to people. Where there is a will there is a way. I sold birds as far away as Australia and slowly grew my business."

In the spring of 1994, Judy received a contract to help jump-start the ostrich production industry in Ontario. "I packed my two daughters in a car, loaded up a trailer with ostriches and drove out there. I loved it."

Although there have certainly been some tough times along the way, Judy hasn't returned to corporate life. She's had a subsequent business partnership unravel and has faced the ongoing challenges of negotiating sales in male-dominated societies like China and Brazil. Nevertheless, Judy now works full-time in her various international marketing ventures, including Agribird, and is happy with her success.

"I'm making a living now. It's not a multi-million dollar living, but it's finally working. I've expanded this year, and I was asked by the government to help develop training for international agricultural trading. This year was the year that I finally decided: 'This is definitely what I want to do.' It's scary, but it's what I want to do."

Through it all, what has she learned? "Get it in writing, trust your gut and just keep going!"

Judy's experiences are indicative of what many entrepreneurs face. Her story helps illustrate why many successful entrepreneurs are individuals who have the ability to deal with cash-flow challenges and business uncertainty, to be inventive and assertive and, above all, to be persistent.

Make a Conscious Choice

Challenges aside, there are plenty of Canadian women contemplating a move in Judy's direction. A recent survey reported that more than two-thirds of the Canadian women executives surveyed were considering leaving their jobs. The reasons they stated were much broader than the stereotypical assumption that they want spend more time with their families. In fact, most of them believed they would find greater financial and non-financial rewards outside of corporate employment.[4]

Colette, a self-employed former executive, put it this way: "I think one of the reasons women are turning to their own businesses in such numbers is because the box that you are put in within a traditional business is just so confining. There is a point that you know you are either going to have to accept being confined or you are going to have to break out and do something for yourself."

Colette chose to step out on her own and to build an environment within which she felt more comfortable. "With my company I wanted to create the kind of place that I wanted to work in, so in terms of values and hierarchy and all of that stuff, the ones here are mine. My company is still small enough that it reflects my values, so internally those corporate issues are not a problem."

Half a decade into her entrepreneurial experience, Colette finds herself happily running a very successful business. Like many women, making a lot of money was not the key motivator in starting her own business.

Colette explains: "If anything, initially I took a hit financially, but my kids were grown up and I had a some money in the bank. I used that freedom to make choices. The business I wanted to start didn't require a lot of capital, so I felt comfortable taking the financial risk. I went into it saying to myself, 'You're not going to make a lot of money, but you are going to have a better life.'

"For the first two years I didn't take a salary at all. Whatever I earned I put back into the company. The third and fourth years I took a salary. I now have a comfortable level of retained earnings. By the third year I actually made as much money as I had made as a corporate executive. I remember thinking, 'Wow, I wouldn't have imagined this!' When I left my job I thought I was walking away from the money. In fact, if you look over my four years as an entrepreneur, I've probably averaged close to what I would have earned if I had stayed in the corporate world."

Colette has definitely succeeded on her own. She has earned business awards and built a solid financial base in her company while working within an environment that suits her values.

We've Got What It Takes

The fact of the matter is that women frequently possess many of the qualities that lead to success as small businesspeople. Multitasking, being willing to start small and grow sensibly, managing a budget, flexibility, commitment and resourcefulness are all characteristics that women entrepreneurs often cite as important to their success. Coincidentally, women also often find themselves well versed in these areas due to experiences they have had as females, wives and mothers.

The results are evident in the success of women-led firms. According to research conducted by the Bank of Montreal, women-led firms are just as financially stable as are male-led firms. They pay their bills on time just as often, and they are just as likely to avoid going out of business. Seventy-six percent of women-led firms running in 1991 were still in business in 1994 versus 78 percent of firms overall. When researchers rated businesses for likelihood of failing in the future due to financial problems, the distribution of scores for women-run firms virtually mirrored that of all firms.[5]

Financial writer Laura Pratt says her research shows that successful women entrepreneurs possess a number of key characteristics. According to Laura, one of the most important success factors is perseverance. "Most of the women I have spoken with told stories centred around the many obstacles they faced, and their success came from their ability to overcome. I don't think that it would be fair to say that that's unique to women, but it is certainly something that women have to contend with as a matter of course, whereas not as many men have had to contend with as many obstacles."

Other skills that are important to success as an entrepreneur, and which women often possess, include the ability to interact effectively with other people and the ability to develop a tough skin. Laura believes the "tough skin" women frequently develop as they progress through life is essential for entrepreneurs "because there are lots of little failures along the way. It's also important for entrepreneurs to have the ability to see the big picture and to understand that there is going to have to be a lot of work put into building their company before good things come out of it. Most entrepreneurs need to have an ability to delay gratification initially."

Never Say Never

One woman who has a great ability to "roll with the punches," and who believes with all her might that she can and will succeed as an entrepreneur, is Natasha. As I've described earlier, Natasha is an amazingly feisty young entrepreneur, who, at age 27, has been in business for herself in one way or another for over a decade.

Natasha's father was killed when she was 10, and this, not surprisingly, led to her fierce level of determination, her strong sense of responsibility and her independent spirit. As the eldest, with a hearing impaired younger brother, Natasha was determined to do her best to help take care of her family.

Natasha started her first job at age 13 as a receptionist for a refrigeration company. With her mother's and principal's blessing, she left school early every day and went to the office. At the ripe old age of 15, Natasha decided to go into business for herself. Starting in the summer and continuing when the school year began, she started a small publishing company called AdverPrizer Magazine and Publishing and opened the Parkavenue Teen Club – a drop-in centre for teens.

In her words, she selected business areas she enjoyed: "I was a natural typist, so that's why I opened the publishing business. That's the key in business – do what you really enjoy because you might do it for free for a while. Also do what you are really good at, use your natural talent."

Natasha published a small magazine and developed brochures, business cards and other advertising tools through AdverPrizer. She did lots of small jobs, but they were all profitable. She worked with what she had and made it work for her. "I didn't spend a lot of money starting these businesses, it took more determination than anything. For my first business I took a small loan from my mom for the computer system, I rented a little office on Main Street and I used equipment that I already had, like my desk."

When she was 17, Natasha and her family moved to St. Albert, Alberta. She continued her entrepreneurial pursuits without missing a beat. "I moved my publishing company with me and I got an incredible account almost the moment I got here. It was the Canadian Association of General Surgeons, and to this day I still work for them. They pay me very well. I do some publishing for them, a lot of computer assistance and quarterly project crunch-time relief. I find that if you just make yourself available, you'll find work. In my case, there was a little ad in the paper for Macintosh computer help. I answered the ad and got the business. It just clicked. I really made the effort to give them a little bit of extra customer service in the beginning, and it turned out well."

Natasha modestly claims that "it just clicked," but her story reflects quite clearly the saying that good luck is nothing but preparedness and opportunity coming together. The fact of the matter is that she took the initiative to win the contract, worked hard to cement the relationship and, as a result, continues to reap the rewards today.

Natasha bought her first home the same year she moved to St. Albert and continued to work hard to develop the skills that she felt she needed in order to pursue her ultimate goal of real estate development and investing. "I had a little subcontract job with computers with the city assessor. I also took courses on real estate and business at night. There was really no room for a social life and that was a sacrifice I was willing to make. I decided to concentrate on furthering myself instead. Low and behold, five years later I met my husband and we were engaged a month after we met. We married a year later.

"My husband and I are very determined, and together we were able to take everything one step further. We bought some investment rental properties and started growing our own little property investments. My boss was buying these condos, so I bought them too. He was very wealthy and obviously knew what he was doing. Actually, he was mad at me for doing that because I was following what he was doing and it was like the old boys club. He didn't want me to profit from his idea; it just wasn't acceptable. He was very upset when I bought 3 condos while he bought 15. I think he thought it was his idea and that I was stealing it."

It seems to me that the thing Natasha's boss was mad about was that Natasha had the sense to know a good idea when she saw one and capitalized on it. Her indomitable spirit prevailed.

"At the same time, my employer started downsizing and I found myself out of work. I decided to start up my company Cream & Sugar – a specialty coffee and tea retail company. It has done well, but it is not huge. It isn't big business, but it allows me to plan for big business. While

I ran Cream & Sugar I started planning a large $1,500,000 property development project."

Here again, Natasha demonstrates her ability to use what she has and to use the smaller opportunities as stepping stones for larger forays. She demonstrates the resourcefulness and stick-to-itiveness so important for success as an entrepreneur.

"The commercial real estate development project was part of the vision I saw for myself when I worked for the City of St. Albert and I saw this property. I started hounding the city almost from that point on. I had this dream of building this big Victorian building that would house my mom's fabric store and other shops and would have some apartment space as well. Finally, the city came and said, 'Okay, we've decided you've bugged us enough, you have two weeks to decide if you want to accept this proposal for the property.' The offer wasn't perfect, but it wasn't bad, and we had the opportunity to take it as is or not. There was a lineup of people wanting this property. So we decided to jump in with both feet, and then we just worked every day until we were done.

"My father-in-law and I jointly acted as the general contractor. He is a builder by trade and worked from a picture and layout that I wanted. I organized the trades and did the interior finishing. As a team we are very good, and that's what it takes – teamwork. All the way along, I always had my mom as a mentor and encourager and we are also a great team. We encourage each other, we get in the occasional argument, but the next day we resolve it. That is very important. We built this together. My parents sold their home and they are taking one of the apartments. We refinanced everything we owned and we got it together and now it is appraised at $1,600,000."

Natasha reflects back on the secrets of her success: "The important thing is that if you have an idea you have to act. If you have an opportunity you have to act on it. A lot of people are afraid to act, they really are. Things do go wrong and you just fix them. With our rental properties we've had one bad tenant and we've had eight good ones. But, yes, we had one bad one and you just fix it. You go and keep going.

"When I make decisions I analyze everything first and then I go with my gut feeling. You have to follow your gut feeling. My mom always says, 'Your instincts are right.' I have been forced into situations where I knew

I should not be going there, but I had to make it work and the alternatives didn't look much better. You have to come up with what you are prepared to accept in terms of your return. For the first 10 years we all starve, but for the next 25 we all retire in the Cayman Islands. You know, it's give and take. You have to give a lot up front and think long term. We had to put all of our capital and all of our assets in and then we'll take the rewards over time. You have to be a long-term thinker. There is never, ever, in my entire experience, a million dollars over night. It just does not happen.

"And it's important to have good people with you. You have to align yourself with great people and you have to take care of them too. That is why I was able to move on, because the people around me encouraged me to do so. I have a best friend who is just wonderful; she is always there. I've also got a great family that encourages me.

"My goal now is to slow down a little because I am expecting a baby. So I'll focus more on managing what we have. We have five rental properties, five commercial spaces and two apartments in our new building, as well as our own house, my mom's business and my own business. That's a lot to manage well. So now, we will grow on a slower basis. The commercial project took a year to plan, and building it took seven months, seven days a week, 10 hours a day. For me a lot of those days were more like 15-hour days. My husband also works full-time elsewhere. We spent all of our holidays here, everything. You need time between things to recuperate and then to plan your next project."

Natasha has certainly earned a reprieve. She is a great example of a natural entrepreneur. She's determined, willing to take risks, trusts her instincts, has clear goals and knows enough to allow others to help her achieve those goals. These are all lessons from which we can all learn, entrepreneurs or not.

Trade-Offs And Pay-Offs

Self-employment can have many rewards, but, as Natasha's story so aptly reflects, it can also be tough sledding. While a significant portion of millionaires earned their money as entrepreneurs, not everyone succeeds financially. And while running your own show can provide extra flexibility with regard to time management, the truth is that many businesspeople report working more hours once they start their own business.

The reality of self-employment is that you trade off one set of work-related costs and benefits for a different, but not necessarily more advantageous, set of costs and benefits. The real question is whether one basket of pros and cons is more appealing to you, given your particular personality and your particular life situation, than another.

Generally, entrepreneurs gain increased schedule flexibility, less exposure to corporate politics, greater ability to influence their work environment and the potential to build long-term equity in a business. There are also many tax advantages to running a small business. If you operate out of your home, then you can deduct the cost of space, business equipment and communications costs from your income. Business-related car and travel expenses can be deducted, and, should you ever sell your business, you may be able to take advantage of the lifetime $500,000 small business capital gains tax exemption.

At the same time, entrepreneurs forego corporate perks like corporate training and health-care spending accounts, and they have the potential for greater isolation and increased stress and uncertainty. Nevertheless, many self-employed women will tell you there isn't another way of earning a living that can match it.

And remember, there probably has never been a better time for Canadian women to set out on their own. Jill, owner of a large bagel cafe chain, expresses it well: "Embrace the fact that you are female. Get out there and find out how much better things are going to be for you because you are female. Be really excited about being a woman at this time in history and treat it as an asset, not a liability.

"A lot of the opportunities that my company has gotten are because I am a woman, and I am perfectly willing to admit that. I've always used it as an advantage rather than a disadvantage. For example, I think women have really great instincts. I think the Canadian business environment today is a wonderful environment within which to be able to draw on a lot of the skills that women have. It is so important to change your mindset and get away from seeing yourself as a victim. You just have to decide that there is nothing that is going to limit your success. Especially in small business!"

The First Step Is the Toughest

For many women, the hardest part was taking the first step. To believe enough in your own abilities and talent to fly without a net takes courage. Sometimes it takes years of contemplation as well.

Sonja took years to make her decision to go solo. "It finally came down to age. My accountant kept saying, 'Well, you really should start this while you are in your forties and not in your fifties. What are you going to do that is going to give you more preparation?'

"I kept thinking I was sort of 'going to school' in the corporate world to get the training to be able to do it on my own. He said, 'Well, yes, you are to a certain extent because all professional experiences are valid. You learn from everything. But if having your own business is your ultimate goal, then what are you waiting for?'

"One thing that I did do, though, that I feel was very useful, was taking a number of small business courses. I also determined whether I had the right skills to start my own business by going to an industrial psychologist, who said to me, 'Look, you need certain kinds of expertise in the following areas: financial management and so on.' So I actively made sure that I got those skills before I set out on my own, and I think this was wise.

"Finally, I weighed the risk. One of the great pieces of advice I got was from a woman who said, 'What's the worst thing that can happen? The worst thing that can happen is that your business doesn't work and then what do you do? Then you find a job.' So once I actually walked through the process of the downside I was comfortable.

"In the end, the whole decision process took a number of years. It also took me a year to actually set up my business – to incorporate, find the right space, think through a business plan, go to the bank and do all of that kind of stuff. I did all of that while I was working. But, at the same time, women that I know and that I see around me running businesses haven't done that and they've been successful. So, I think it just depends on who you are and how comfortable you are with risk."

Sonja's story illustrates a key point. Probably the biggest impediment to women stepping out on their own is the fear of taking a risk. Sometimes overcoming it just requires one more instance of working for an incompetent boss or dropping off your screaming child at the babysitter. Sometimes the decision gets made for you through job loss. However it happens, more and more women are finding career fulfillment through entrepreneurial means. If you think it may be the right path for you too, then I wholeheartedly encourage you to explore this avenue further. The worst that can happen is that it doesn't work for you and you go back to working for someone else. The best that could happen is beyond your wildest imagination. So consider taking a risk and betting on you, because if you're not going to, who else will?

What limiting beliefs do you have about your worthiness? It's time to change those negative messages and replace them with the positive feedback that will allow you to achieve your full financial potential regardless of who signs your paycheque. Self-employment is just one of the infinite number of career options available to you.

Let us celebrate all women entrepreneurs for taking charge of their power to shape their own path and define their own success. And let's be especially proud of those women who have given themselves the permission to accept financial success and the leadership role that often accompanies being a financially powerful woman.

Making It Happen – Getting Past the Fear of Running Your Own Show

If you think you may have what it takes to start your own business but have been held back by fear, now is the time to take a closer look at your fear. What is the honest to goodness worst thing that could happen if you pursued your business vision? What are you really afraid of? Close you eyes and think about this for the next 5 or 10 minutes. Then write down all of the fears that come to mind.

I am afraid that the following things might happen if I pursue my entrepreneurial dream:

____

____

____

____

____

____

Now ask yourself, what is the percentage probability of each of the fears listed above actually happening if you pursue your dream? Write a percentage probability next to each fear above. Then circle the fears with the highest percentage likelihood and the ones you just couldn't accept having happen. Use the space below to list ways you could reduce the risk of these "monster fears" actually occurring. For instance, if one of your greatest fears is that your business would go bankrupt, then you might list the following ideas to minimize the risk of this happening:

- Find a partner with the skills I lack
- Save an additional $10,000 to help me through low cash-flow periods
- Set up the business while continuing to work part-time in the corporate world
- Don't leave my current job until I actually land my first entrepreneurial sale
- Take business management classes in those areas in which I am weak
- Do more research and planning for my business idea
- Minimize start-up costs by initially running my business from home
- Set profit goals for years one and two of operation. If the goals aren't met, then I will exit the business and return to working for someone else.

Ways to reduce my risk:

What steps can you take now to move closer to that vision? Are there specific skills you could improve by taking courses? Are there people who work in the industry in which you are interested with whom you could have lunch and ask for advice? Are you ready to put your idea on paper in the form of a business plan? Are you ready to apply for financing? Whatever it is, commit to taking one more specific step towards you vision in the next 12 months. Write down what that step will be in the space that follows.

I commit to undertaking the following step towards my own business vision within the next 12 months:

12

It's Easier Than You Think

Few things are of themselves impossible, and we lack
the application to make them a success rather than the means.
KENNETH PRATT

You have now reached the third stage of the prosperity equation – investing your savings for maximum return. This section of the book is focused on the nuts and bolts of investing. You will learn all you need to know to develop a personal investment plan. We'll cover the differences between investments such as stocks, bonds, mutual funds and real estate, the best mix of investments for you and how to put it all together into your own personal investment plan. By the end of this section you'll be well equipped to manage your money effectively, and I think you'll be amazed at how much simpler it is than the financial experts often lead you to believe.

A word of caution, this section of the book may seem a little dry at times (finance can be like that), but once you put this information into action and your assets begin to multiply, it will all become much more interesting. Of that, I can assure you.

If You Can Bake a Cake, Then You Can Manage Your Money

Right now you may think financial management and investing is complex, confusing and over your head. If you feel this way strongly, then you probably think that whatever you do with your money is not the best thing to be doing and, as a result, you avoid doing anything until you absolutely have to. This only increases your level of anxiety and makes the whole process frustrating. For you, money management may well equal frustration with a capital "F."

It really is easier than you think. The stock market is really no different than a farmers market except that instead of carrots you barter for shares of Coca-Cola and Microsoft. Moreover, there are only four basic forms of investment that you need to know about (near-cash, stocks, bonds and mutual funds). Exotic investment vehicles like futures, derivatives and strip bonds are to investing what leeks and fennel are to healthy eating. In other words, if you want to get exotic you can, but you certainly do not have to; you can accomplish everything you want to within your financial plan without fancy hybrid investments. For the sake of simplicity, we'll stick to the mainstream investments.

When it comes right down to it, investing is just like baking a cake. You start by selecting the right ingredients in the form of investments. You measure them and mix them together in the right proportions to match your personal risk profile. Then you put it all in the oven and wait. In the end, you enjoy a scrumptious dessert in the form of the positive benefits you are able to enjoy due to your careful investing.

Piggy Banks of All Sorts – Basic Financial Investment Options

Let's start by reviewing each of the basic types of financial investment. Of course, you can also invest in physical assets like real estate, which we will cover in Chapter 16, but let's start with the basic financial investments.

Cash and Near-Cash Investments

These investments are practically the same as keeping cash in your pocket except that they provide a modest return in the form of interest. Cash and near-cash investment vehicles include bank accounts and money market funds. They offer low returns (low interest) but are highly liquid. Liquidity refers to how easy it is for you to gain access to your money when it is invested. It is the high liquidity of cash and near-cash investments that is their primary benefit.

Money market funds differ slightly from keeping your money in the bank. In a money market fund your money is pooled with the money from all of the investors in the fund. Essentially, the fund manager uses this money to make very safe short-term loans to governments and companies. Because your money is pooled with lots of other people's money you don't need to worry about when the loans come due before withdrawing your share of the cash. This is because there are so many loans in the pool that many of them are coming due every day. Furthermore, the money market fund manager keeps some extra cash on hand at all times. As a result, you can sell your money market investment any time you want and get back your money plus your share of the interest earned on the loans.

All you really need to remember, from an investment point of view, is that investing in a money market fund is like keeping money in your bank account except that the interest you earn might be slightly higher than what your bank pays. Cash and near-cash investments, including money market funds, are low-risk investments with safe, low returns.

Bonds

Corporate bonds are certificates issued by companies that promise to repay, with specified timing, the money that the investor – or bondholder – has loaned to them. In return for use of the investor's money, the company also pays interest on the loan. The bondholder does not have any ownership in the company and generally does not have any voting rights on company matters, nor does she receive dividends. Her sole form of compensation is interest paid on the bond.

Government bonds are essentially the same as corporate bonds except that various levels of government issue them. You can purchase bonds issued by the federal government, provincial government or municipalities.

Certificates of deposit (CDs) are basically the same as government bonds except that they are usually issued by financial institutions. Guaranteed investment certificates (GICs) and treasury bills (T-bills) are also certificates of loan that pay interest for the use of your money. All of these types of investments, in which you are essentially lending money to the issuer of the investment, can be referred to as debt instruments.

Not all bonds and debt instruments are considered low-risk investments. Some bonds are offered from companies that are in precarious financial situations. This means that there is a higher chance that the company will go bankrupt and be unable to pay back the money you lent it by buying its bond. The riskiest of these bonds are sometimes referred to as junk bonds. In this case, the bonds are clearly identified as such by their bond rating. A bond rating is the rating assigned to the bond by one of the bond rating agencies. In Canada, the bond rating agencies include Canadian Bond Rating Service and Dominion Bond Rating Service; in the U.S. they include Moody's, and Standard and Poor's. Bonds are rated from the safest level to the riskiest level. For example, Canadian Bond Rating Service uses ratings from the top rating of A++, to A+, to A, to B++ and so on down to C and D. Generally, if you are looking for a very safe investment, then you don't want to buy any bonds with a rating below B++.

To sum up, bonds come in all levels of risk, but the majority of bonds issued by various levels of the Canadian government and well-known large companies carry very little risk of losing money. In addition, they generally pay higher interest rates than do near-cash investments in order to compensate the bondholder for giving up access to her money for a longer period of time.

As an investor you can choose to buy bonds directly or you can buy shares of a bond fund. If you buy bonds directly, then you decide on what maturity date you are looking for and ask your broker what is available. This way, if you hold the bond until it matures, you know from the outset exactly how much the interest payments will be and exactly how much you will get back when this occurs. You also avoid paying the annual management fee that bond fund managers charge and that usually averages around 1.5 percent of your total investment each year. The downside is that you have to select your own bonds, and if you end up selling before the bond matures, the market value of your bond may be less than you actually invested, with the result that you may lose some of your initial investment.

On the other hand, if you buy into a bond fund, the bond manager will do the work of selecting credit-worthy bonds. You can take your money out any time, but again the amount you receive will depend on the market value of the bonds held by the fund on that date. Thus, you can't predict the exact return you will make. Personally, I suggest that novice bond investors invest in bond funds rather than in individual bonds. Soon I will explain how to do this.

One factor to keep in mind when choosing between CDs, GICs and T-bills versus bonds is that CDs, GICs and T-bills generally cannot be sold or cashed in before their maturity date, whereas this is not true of bonds. At the same time, just because you can sell a bond before it matures doesn't mean you will necessarily get the price you want for it. The selling price depends on how much the remaining bond interest payments are worth to potential buyers. Since you are selling a stream of future interest payments plus a lump-sum payback of the principal invested at some point in the future, the price buyers are willing to pay depends on how much they can earn on alternative investments with similar levels of risk.

For example, say you are selling a bond that will pay out eight percent of its face value of $100 plus the original $100 investment when it matures in 12 months. Buyers will be willing to pay more than the original $100 you invested if interest rates have fallen since your purchase and they can no longer buy a one-year bond with the same level of risk that offers an eight percent annual return. If the same company that sold you your eight percent bond is now only offering seven percent interest on its new one-year bonds, then buyers should be willing to pay you up to $100.93 for your bond. At any price up to $100.93, the buyer will make at least as high a return on her investment as she would make if she bought the new one-year seven percent bond. So if interest falls, then your bond's market value rises. If interest rates rise, though, your bond, with its fixed interest payments, becomes less valuable than alternative investments and its market value falls.

So while bonds can offer more flexibility than other near-cash interest-paying investments (in that you are more likely to be able to sell them before they mature), the price you can sell them for also fluctuates, depending on how interest rates move in the market overall.

Stocks

The terms "stocks" and "shares" refer to basically the same thing – part ownership of the company that issued them. So if you hear one person use the term "stocks" and another use the term "shares," then you know that they are talking about the same thing. There are two types of stock: common stock and preferred stock. The only difference is that a share refers to a single unit, whereas the term "stock" can be used to refer to a single unit of ownership or the entire pool of shares of a company.

Common Stock

Owning common stock actually means you own a portion of the company that issued the stock. If you own stock in Coca-Cola, then you, along with all of the other shareholders, own part of the company.

Each day the stock price is determined through the barter system on the stock market. In other words, the stock price is determined by supply and demand. If the company is doing well, then it is likely that the demand for its stock will rise as investors decide to buy some. At the same time, the existing investors won't sell until the price offered by the new investors is as high as they think their share of the company is worth. So in a continual process, the highest price offered by new investors is matched up with the lowest price a seller is willing to take, and stock changes hands. Overall, the stock prices change each day, and throughout the day, based on bartering between stockbrokers representing buyers and sellers at the stock exchange. In simplified terms, if a lot of people want a particular company's stock, then the price is likely to rise; if fewer people want to buy than sell, then the price is bound to fall. It's just like the price of carrots at the farmers market.

Besides making money on a stock investment by buying at a lower price than that at which you eventually sell, you may also receive dividends while you own the stock. Many companies choose to pay out a portion of their company profits – as dividends – to shareholders. Usually the companies pay the same level of dividends at the same times each year, so dividend income is fairly predictable. As an investor you can choose to have dividends automatically reinvested in more of the company's stock or have them paid to you directly in cash.

As a partial owner of the company, you also have the right to vote in the election of its board of directors and any other important matters that are put to a shareholders' vote. In order to allow you to make an informed decision when casting your vote, companies are required by law to send you a proxy statement. A proxy statement is nothing more than an information brochure that provides background information on the matter that is being taken to a vote.

Generally, you will not have to vote very often. This tends to be a very minor investment task. Since, typically, every share counts as one vote, the largest shareholders often determine what ultimately happens. Nevertheless, everyone with share ownership does have the opportunity to cast his or her vote.

Another thing to keep in mind is that in the event that the company you own stock in goes bankrupt, you, the common shareholder, will be the last person who gets paid back for your investment. In other words, the employees must receive wages owed, the other parties the business owed money to must be paid back, the bondholders must be paid back and then the preferred shareholders must be paid back. Last of all, any remaining money is divided among the common shareholders. However, the risk of bankruptcy is very low for most "mainstream" or "blue chip" stocks. If you buy stocks in large, long-standing companies that are listed on the larger stock exchanges, such as the Toronto Stock Exchange or the New York Stock Exchange, then it is unlikely you will lose money due to one of them going bankrupt. So if you stick to blue chip stocks, then you needn't lose a lot of sleep over the risk of bankruptcy (even though the occasional blue chip stock, like Eaton's, does end up losing a significant portion of its value in a short period of time).

In sum, common stock comes in all levels of risk, and it is up to the buyer to decide how risky she thinks a specific stock is and whether she thinks the price of that stock will go up or down in the future. The other factor to consider in estimating the investment's expected return is how much dividend income you expect to be paid.

PREFERRED STOCK

Preferred stock is stock that has special features over and above the common stock of the same issuing company. Usually these special features involve some combination of more extensive voting rights and higher dividends. Furthermore, in the event of bankruptcy, preferred shareholders have a higher priority claim against the proceeds of the company's assets than do the common shareholders.

Stock Options

Stock options are options to buy or sell shares at a specified price at a later date in time. These investment tools are rather complex and are not generally used by the average investor. I would strongly suggest that you avoid them until you are very sophisticated in your knowledge and have a large amount of time to devote to your investment activity.

The Biggest Piggy Banks in the World – Mutual Funds

You can either buy all of the types of investments described above directly or you can buy them indirectly through a mutual fund. The basic idea behind mutual funds is that a lot of small investors can pool their money together and have it invested by a professional fund manager on their behalf.

There are two primary benefits that mutual funds have and that direct ownership does not have. First, you get the benefit of a mutual fund manager watching the market and making the investment decisions on a day-to-day basis. If she is a good manager, then this service is worth the management fees the fund charges you. For stock-based mutual funds these fees typically total about two percent of your total investment each year.

The second benefit of mutual funds is diversification. Because the money of many investors is pooled together in the fund, the fund manager has the ability to invest it across a number of different individual stocks and bonds. This reduces your overall risk, since you are not "putting all of your eggs in one basket." If one of the individual stocks in the basket takes a dive, then you still have the others to count on.

Because of these two significant advantages, mutual funds are usually the initial way investors enter the market. And this is the way

I would suggest you enter the stock market if you are not already involved in it.

Mutual Fund Types

There are hundreds of different mutual funds from which to choose.

- **Money market funds** were described above. They are the lowest-risk mutual funds but also offer fairly low returns – usually about the same as the rate of interest banks pay on savings accounts. These mutual funds are invested in short-term, high-quality, bond-type investments. Since they rarely have any commissions associated with buying or selling, money market funds can be a good place to put money that you want easy access to in the short run. However, you won't earn much more interest on this money than you would if it was in your bank account.
- **Income funds** invest in companies that pay above average dividends or in bond type securities that make regular interest payments. Income funds tend to be more predictable in returns (less risky), but the potential upside is also more limited than it is for the riskier funds, such as growth funds. Income funds are more risky than money market funds but less risky than growth funds.
- **Balanced funds** invest in a mix of stocks, bonds and money market funds. They are kind of middle-of-the-road funds in terms of risk and return. Balanced fund managers switch the percentage invested in the fund between stocks, bonds and money market, depending on how well they think each type of investment will do in the near future.
- **Growth funds** focus on buying high growth-potential companies that have a high level of potential risk associated with them. The prices of these stocks are expected to fluctuate over time, but over the long run the returns are expected to be high in order to compensate for the risk of fluctuation. Of course there are no guarantees, so investing in growth mutual funds is more risky than is investing in money market, income and balanced funds.
- **Industry-sector funds** focus on investing within a specific industry sector, such as health care or banking. You may want to chose industry-sector funds if you feel certain that a particular sector of the economy is going to perform strongly over your investment horizon, but you don't want to place a bet on one or more individual stocks within the sector. For example, I believe that the pharmaceutical sector will do well as baby boomers continue to age, but I

don't personally know which pharmaceutical company will hit the jackpot with the right drug discoveries. For this reason, I invest in a pharmaceutical-focused mutual fund that buys stocks in numerous different drug companies on my behalf.

- **Index funds** promise you the same return as does the stock market index that you read about in the newspaper or hear about on the news. When you hear that the TSE 300 rose one percent today, the newscaster is saying that the total price of 300 specific stocks that make up the TSE 300 index was one percent higher at the end of the day today than it was at the end of the day yesterday. The TSE 300 does not have all of the stocks that are listed on the Toronto Stock Exchange; rather, it contains a fairly representative group of stocks and provides an indication of the overall direction of stock prices in Canada. Index funds produce the same price increases or decreases as does the index because they are invested in the same stocks as is the index, and in the same proportions.
- **Global funds** invest outside of Canada. They can provide you with diversification across countries. Under current RRSP rules, however, you can only invest a maximum of 20 percent of your total RRSP in foreign content. If you wanted to buy more than 20 percent, then you would have to buy the additional foreign investment outside of your RRSP and pay taxes on your gains each time you sell one of these investments.
- **Real Estate Investment Trusts** (REITs) are investment pools that are like mutual funds except that, rather than buying stocks or bonds with the money in the fund, the investment manager invests in real estate. A REIT can buy a number of hotels and commercial office towers, for instance, and, as an REIT investor, you can own a portion of that real estate.

In addition to the basic investment types listed above, new hybrid investments combining components of various forms of investments are continuously being invented. For example, you can now buy GICs with interest rates that are linked to the performance of the stock market. They offer the GIC protection of your initial investment but add a modest stock market risk component in determining the interest payout. Guaranteed Investment Funds (GIFs) are similar in that their value 10 years after you buy them is guaranteed to be at least as much as it was on the date of your original purchase.† However, through the GIF your money is actually invested in mutual funds so that you also have the potential upside of returns that are linked to the growth in value of the mutual fund assets. These are just a couple of examples of the multitude of investment alternatives now available. The bottom line is that if the investment in question offers benefits that are attractive to you and you understand exactly what you are getting into, consider investing. However, if you aren't completely comfortable with the product, stick to the basic investment products that we've discussed.

Now that you've read this chapter, you are aware of all of the different financial assets that you need to know about to be a successful investor. You don't need to jump into all of them all at once, nor should you. As you develop your personal investment plan through the next few chapters you will be able to pick a few investment areas and begin investing with a simple monthly withdrawal from your bank account. As you become more experienced at investing, these terms, which may seem confusing now, will become second nature to you.

Making It Happen – Mastering the Basic Financial Jargon

Before you go on, make sure you can explain what the following terms mean. If you cannot do so, you may wish to review this chapter one more time before proceeding.

1. Money Market Fund:

____

2. Bond:

____

† It's really not much of a guarantee. You'd have to have a number of poor investments within a diversified portfolio in order to end up with less value at the end of 10 years than when you started.

3. Common Stock:

____

4. Preferred Stock:

____

5. Share:

____

6. Dividend:

____

7. Proxy Statement:

____

8. Liquidity:

____

9. Return:

____

10. Diversification:

____

11. TSE 300 Index:

____

12. Stock Exchange:

____

13

Basic Training I

Unless you enter the tiger's den you cannot take the cubs.

Japanese Proverb

There are only a few basic principles of investing that you really need to understand in order to make informed investments. The three fundamental principles of investing covered in this chapter are these.

1. A dollar today is worth more than it will be tomorrow.
2. The riskier the investment, the higher the anticipated payoff.
3. Diversification is a cost-free way to lower your investment risk.

But first, I'd like to share some of what I experienced when I tried to educate myself about investing. Maybe you can relate to this.

It took me almost four years from when I first started thinking about investing some of my savings in the stock market until I actually did so. When I first started making inquiries, I had just finished my undergraduate degree in university and had $10,000 in savings. I went to see a stockbroker whom I found in the phone book. He met with me, answered my questions, confused me, scared me and sent me away with a paperback on investing. Then, when I casually asked my uncle about the stock market, he said, "You don't want to invest any money in the stock market that you are not prepared to lose," so I dropped the subject. I hadn't worked my butt off to save $10,000 just to gamble it away at the roulette table, and that was the impression of the stock market that I was getting. Years later, I now know that careful investing in the stock market is nothing like stepping up to the roulette table, and I wish I'd started buying stocks a lot sooner.

Why do I wish I had started investing in the stock market sooner? Because the way investing often works is that the more risk you have of your investment going down a lot, the more chance you have of it going up a lot. Historically, over the long term, the stock market, with its higher level of risk, has outperformed less risky investments such as bonds, and for that reason many people are willing to risk owning stocks.

You may or may not be a prime candidate for stock investing. It depends on how much investment risk is suitable for your personal circumstances and how soon you need access to your money. But before we go into all of that, let's step back and talk about what determines the return you can expect to make from different types of investments. It all comes down to two basic factors – how long your money is tied up and how much variability there is in the amount you will ultimately earn from the investment. In other words, the longer your have to give up access to your money, the higher the return should be; and the bigger the range in what you could end up earning from your investment, the higher the most likely "expected return" should be. These are the two primary factors that affect the expected return of any financial investment you make, regardless of whether it is in the stock market or elsewhere. Let's go through each in detail.

A Dollar Today Is Worth More Than a Dollar Tomorrow

Let's first deal with the time factor. The time value of money refers to the principle that a specific amount of money, such as a $10 bill, is worth more today than it will be in the future. This is because if you have access to the money today, then you have the opportunity to use it to invest in something that could theoretically be worth more tomorrow than it is today. For example, you might use the money to buy the ingredients to bake a cake today and sell it at a profit tomorrow. Without access to the money to buy the ingredients, you could not have baked the cake and would have missed out on this profit opportunity.

When you lend money to banks in the form of bank deposits, to governments in the form of government bonds or to companies in the form of corporate bonds, part of the interest you earn is compensation for providing the use of your money. In the form of interest, the borrowers pay you a portion of the profit they expect to make on whatever they use your money for.

More specifically, when you lend a bank money in the form of a deposit, the bank then lends it to other people at a higher interest rate. One way the bank makes money is by pocketing the difference between the higher interest rate it charges borrowers and the lower interest rate it pays depositors (or lenders). Likewise, the corporation you lend money to (by buying a corporate bond) will typically use your money to invest in expansion, since its management believes they can make more money by expanding the business than it costs them to borrow from you. In other words, they may believe they can earn a 10% return using the money they are paying you 6% on and will be able to pocket the difference. Hence, part of the return you expect from any investment is for providing the use of your money over time.

The Higher the Risk, the Higher the Expected Return

The second factor influencing the investment return promised to you is the risk that you may not get as much money out of the investment as you expected. For one thing, with any investment there is always a risk that the entity you are allowing to use your money will go bankrupt and that, therefore, you might lose some or all of the money you put into the investment. In many investments this risk is minuscule and people don't think about it. Bank deposits, for instance, are extremely low-risk in this regard, since Canada's major banks are very strong and highly unlikely to go bankrupt. Furthermore, the Canadian government guarantees that in the event that any registered bank in Canada goes bankrupt, the government will ensure that all depositors get back their deposits up to a maximum of $60,000 per person, per financial institution.

Essentially, in all but the most speculative of investments, such as junk bonds or penny stock,† the risk of bankruptcy is negligible.

The other part of risk to your initial, or "principal," investment is that its value may fluctuate in the resale market due to supply and demand. If your investment is one in which using a resale market, like a stock exchange, is the only way you can get your money out of the investment, then you need to be concerned with how strong you expect the demand for your investment to be in the future. For example, you may own some common stock that other investors considered attractive, and the resultant strong demand from buyers pushes up the price being paid in the stock market. Likewise, if people who own the stock want to sell more of it than other people want to buy, then the price will be bid down until there is a balance between supply and demand. At this point you will not be able to sell your stock for as much as you initially paid for it.

As I said before, the investment market is no different than a farmers market. If only one farmer has tomatoes to sell and all the shoppers want to buy tomatoes, then the seller can raise the price until supply equals demand. On the other hand, if 20 farmers show up with truckloads of tomatoes, then prices will be cut and the tomatoes will sell for less.

So, if there is less demand for your investment when you want to sell it than there was when you bought it, you will end up selling it for a lower price than you bought it for and, as a result, will lose some of your initial investment principal. On the other hand, if demand has increased more than supply when you sell, then you will be able to sell for a higher price than you bought at and, as a result, you will make money on your investment. You will make a positive investment return.

The trick is to invest in things that you think will generate positive investment returns. This means picking investments that you think will be in greater demand in the future than they are now. Shortly, we'll cover how to do that. First, however, let's go back to risk for a minute.

† Penny stock is in an unproven venture, where the price per share is usually under $5.00. It is only traded on the smallest stock exchanges or outside of stock exchanges altogether.

Risk Is Another Word for Volatility

If something is volatile, then it is likely to change rapidly and unpredictably. When people refer to an investment as high-risk, they are really saying that its value is highly volatile. For example, Internet-related stocks, like Yahoo! and AOL and bid.com, are high-risk investments. The share price of these stocks increases and decreases by large percentages from one day to the next, since investors as a whole keep changing their minds about how much they think the companies are worth and, therefore, how much they are willing to pay for the stock. One day everyone wants to own a piece of the Internet action because the Internet "is the wave of the future," and the next day people change their minds because a new report is released that shows that "none of the Internet companies are profitable." Some investors who buy at the right time and sell at the right time become millionaires, while others lose their shirts.

The point is, all investments have some level of risk associated with them, and the more risky an investment is, the wider the swings in value are expected to be. The problem is that if you want to make higher returns on your investments over time, then you have to be prepared to take on some risk. If you only invest in the lowest-risk investments, like guaranteed investment certificates, then you will earn a predictable but low return. If you invest in riskier investments, like stocks, then you have the possibility of earning a higher return, but you also have more potential to lose money.

Historically, over the long run, averaging out all of the ups and downs in value, stock investors have usually earned higher returns than have non-stock investors. In other words, even with big drops in the stock market, like the "crashes" of 1929 and 1987, over the long haul the stock market has still provided higher investment returns than have low-risk investments. For example, from 1956 to 1996, the TSE 300 Index increased an average of 10 percent each year, while the average returns an investor earned on long-term government bonds was 8.6 percent.[2] In the chart below, I have plotted the TSE 300 returns for the last 10 years versus the rate you would earn by holding five-year GICs.[3]

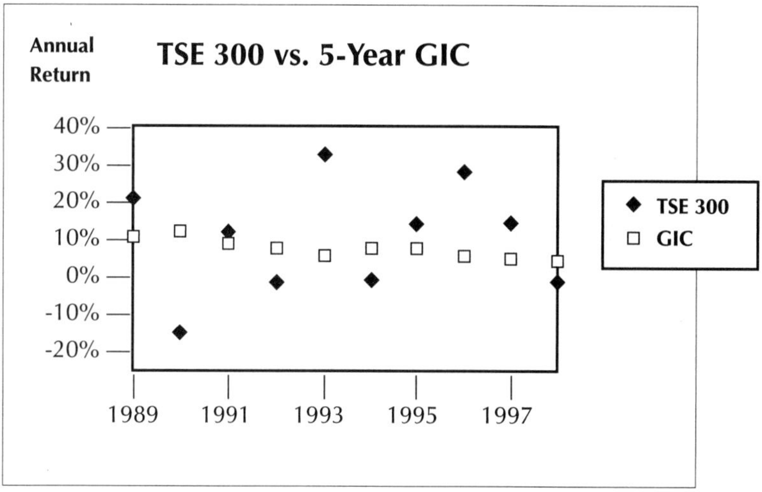

As you can see, more often than not the stock market returns were higher than the GIC returns, but they varied much more from year to year. In 1990, the TSE 300 investors would have lost close to 15 percent of the value of their investments. On the other hand, if they held onto their stock throughout the 10 years, then they came out ahead of the GIC investors. Over the full 10 years, five-year GICs returns worked out to 7.7 percent per year, while the TSE 300 returned an annual compound rate of 10.6 percent. The difference between these two rates of return may not seem worth the risk of losing 15 percent of your money from one year to the next. However, as the following chart shows, if you invested $10,000 at the beginning of 1989 in both, then you would end up with $20,949 from the GIC investment and $25,109 from the TSE 300 investment.

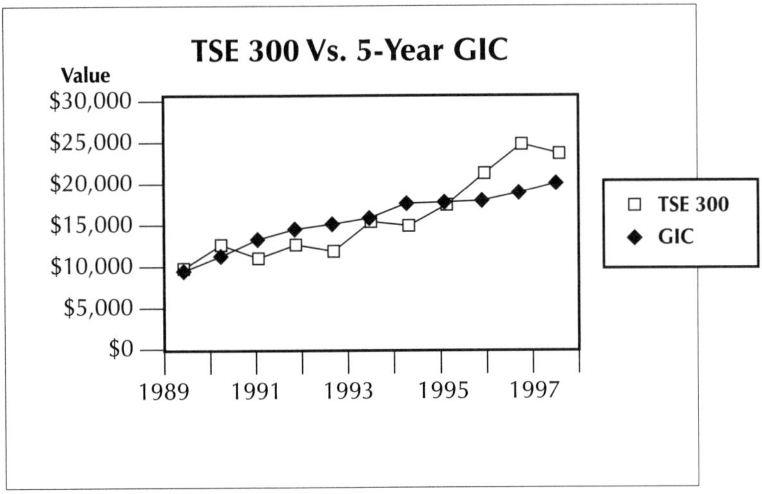

Another way to look at it is to consider the "Rule of 72," which tells you how quickly your money will double depending on what interest rate it earns. To do the calculation you divide 72 by the percentage rate of return earned each year. So if you invest $10,000 at 7.7 percent it will double every 9.4 years (72 ÷ 7.7 = 9.4); invested at 10.6 percent it will double in 6.8 years (72 ÷ 10.6 = 6.8). Just a small percentage difference in annual returns adds up to a significant difference in value over time.

In the U.S., the performance of the stock market has been even better than it has in Canada. In that market you can choose any 20-year period between 1802 and 1999, and when you compare the return on the stock market to that of any other financial investment, the stock market return is almost always higher.[4]

In Canada, stocks have generally performed better than non-equity investments over the long run. However, in the short run, this has not always been the case. Here, there have been several 10-year periods when medium-term bonds have done better than stocks, and there have even been a few 10-year spans in which near-cash investments have outperformed stocks.[5]

This explains why, even with the stock market's high long-term performance record, investors invest in other assets besides stock. Most people don't have the stomach to ride the stock market roller coaster with all of their money. None of us can predict the future perfectly, and, thus, we can't predict the precise value that our stock market investments will be worth on the future date at which we sell them. So if all of a sudden we need cash tomorrow and the stock market happens to be down, then we may end up selling at a loss.

Likewise, no one can predict how and when the stock market, or the value of the individual stocks that are traded on the stock market, will fluctuate. As you read and gather more information about the stock market you will notice that every time the past performance of a stock or a mutual fund is reported, the disclaimer "past performance does not predict future performance," or some variation of it, will appear. This is because all of the analysis that says that the stocks, on average, provide investors with a better long-term return than other financial investments is based on historical analysis. History suggests that this trend is pretty consistent, and so we assume that it will continue in the future. But the fact of the matter is that no one can guarantee this. Hence, investing in the stock market involves taking a risk. The question you need to ask yourself, in developing your own investment portfolio, is how much risk you are willing to take. But remember that if you aren't willing to take on any risk, then you won't earn returns much higher than the rate of inflation.

The overall message I want to convey is that although the stock market can be daunting, a gradual, careful entry into it can be a very effective way for you to share in the benefits that until recently were only enjoyed by the wealthy. Between 1993 and 1996, the total value of equities, or stocks, on the Toronto Stock Exchange doubled, from a total value of $150 billion to $300 billion. However, the typical stockholder was still male, in his forties, university-educated and with a higher than average income. Wealthy households are the big winners; over 70 percent of Canadian households with yearly incomes of at least $75,000 own stock.[6]

The majority of Canadians still don't own any stock. In 1996, only 37 percent of Canadian adults owned stock either directly or indirectly through mutual funds or pension plans.[7] Women, more than men, tend to shy away from investing in stock. You may find though, as you create your personal risk profile in this chapter's "Making It Happen" exercise, that a certain amount of stock ownership makes sense for you.

ALWAYS DIVERSIFY

Diversification is an extremely important concept, which we touched on earlier when discussing mutual funds. Let's review it one more time. Essentially, diversifying means not putting all of your eggs in one basket. It is as simple as that. When it comes to investments it refers to buying investments with different types of risk. By doing this you actually reduce your overall chances of ending up with a really big loss because it is not likely that all of your investments will go down at the same time. Some may go down while others go up, but when you add it all together you typically end up earning a higher return than would have been the case had you put all of your money into a lower-risk investment. In other words, diversification allows you to reduce the volatility of your investment portfolio without necessarily reducing the overall expected return.

Diversification works because the prices of different companies' stock do not move exactly together. When one stock is going down, others are not necessarily going down as well. By buying a number of stocks, instead of just one, you reduce the risk in your investment portfolio related specifically to changes that only affect individual stocks. This is sometimes referred to as "unique risk." For example, Mining Company ABC may end up having its stock price fall 50 percent after a freak accident causes the cave-in of the company's largest mine. This accident directly affects Mining Company ABC, but it does not directly affect any other stocks. If you had all of your money invested in Mining Company ABC, then you would immediately lose 50 percent of the value of your investment. If, instead, your investments were equally divided across 10 stocks, then the value of your total portfolio would only decline 5 percent, since Mining Company ABC only makes up 10 percent of your portfolio.

The risk that diversification does not reduce is "market risk." Market risk refers to risks that are likely to affect many or all stocks at the same time. For instance, when various Asian economies experienced severe economic difficulties in the late summer of 1998, the prices of many Canadian stocks fell. Much of this was due to the dependence of many of these Canadian companies on export sales to Asia. Furthermore, investor nervousness meant that many investors shifted their money from stocks to other types of assets, thus further reducing the demand for stocks and causing the prices to fall. In the end, the TSE 300 Index fell from a high of 7,835 in April 1998 to a low of 5,325 in early October 1998. Much of this fluctuation reflects market risk – risk that cannot be eliminated through diversification.

Generally the stock market suffers a "correction" every few years. A correction is defined as a drop of over 10 percent in the overall value. For instance, between 1969 and 1999, the Canadian stock market had nine market corrections.[8]

Keep in mind, though, that over the long run, through all the ups and downs along the way, investing in common stock has still delivered much higher average returns to investors than have other lower-risk investments. Returning to the 1998 example, the TSE 300 Index was back up to 6,485 by the end of 1998. Stock market investors are willing to accept market risk and the chance of losses in the short term; they expect to be rewarded with higher average returns in the long term. So far, since our stock market has been in existence, this has generally been the case.

In the table below, you can see that the average annual return on common stock is almost six percent higher than the average return on the very low-risk investment of treasury bills. With T-bills you know how much interest you will be paid and you never earn any more or any less; instead, the buying power of the money you have invested just keeps pace with inflation. On the other hand, with common stock some years you end up with higher returns on your investment and sometimes with lower returns. But one thing is certain: if you have invested in stock instead of T-bills over the past many years, then you are very likely to have come out ahead.

Historical Canadian Investment Returns (1950-1995)[9]

Investments	Average Annual Return to Investor
Common Stocks	12.0%
Long-term Government Bonds	7.4%
Treasury Bills	6.4%
Inflation	4.4%

No matter what you buy in your investment portfolio, as long as you have any sort of investments other than those with no risk whatsoever (like T-bills or Canada Savings Bonds), then you should diversify. If you own stocks of any type, corporate bonds of any type or more complex financial investment products, then you should reduce your overall portfolio risk by diversifying and spreading your money across a number of investments.

Ways to Diversify

It is very important that you diversify. As I said before, diversification is a no-cost way to lower your risk, and there is absolutely no reason not to take advantage of it. However, you have to do it correctly in order for it to work.

Carol explains how she thought she was diversifying by buying a number of GICs. "When I first started saving, I put all of my money in GICs because the interest rates were high and they were safe investments. I thought I was diversifying because I bought them at a couple of different banks, but they were still all bank GICs, so I really wasn't diversified at all, I just thought I was."

Carol now understands that buying a number of investments that are exactly the same as each other, except for being offered by different financial institutions, is not what diversifying is all about. Now an active 70-year-old investor with a sizable portfolio, she understands that diversification refers to buying various types of investments, and she has a portfolio containing GICs, bonds, mutual funds and stocks in various industry sectors.

So how do you diversify effectively? Well, first you need to recognize that there are three major areas that you can diversify across – all of which will help to lower your investment portfolio risk.

1. Diversify across asset types

First, diversify across asset types. This means that unless you are absolutely risk-averse and plan only to invest in the safest of assets (T-bills, government bonds and short-term GICs), then you should put your savings into a mix of investment types. For most people, this means a mix of safe investments such as the ones I just listed, some longer-term interest-bearing investments such as corporate bonds and some higher-risk/higher-expected-return equity investments such as common stocks and/or equity-based mutual funds. You may also decide to augment your investments with other non-financial investments such as real estate.

2. Diversify across industry sectors

The next area of diversification to consider is across industries. In other words, if you have stocks in your portfolio that are from 10 different companies but all of the companies are in the automotive industry, you have not diversified across industries. As a result, your portfolio will be very vulnerable to "industry-specific risk." For example, if a new form of transportation is invented tomorrow by a new breed of non-combustion engine makers, then all of the traditional automotive companies and their suppliers could be adversely affected. Thus, all of the stock in your portfolio would be likely to fall in value at the same time. In this case you have a high level of industry-specific risk in your portfolio.

Likewise, you also don't want to concentrate your money solely in an investment whose value is all highly dependent on one driving factor. For example, you don't want to only invest in investments that are strongly affected by interest rates, since they will all move up and down together. Instead, you could invest in stock across various relatively unrelated industries, such as the manufacturing industry, the financial industry, the retail industry and all industries as a whole. While falling interest rates tend to be good for both the manufacturing industry and the financial industry, they don't have any significant impact on the retail industry or all industries as a whole.

You can achieve industry diversification relatively easily by investing in different mutual funds, with each focusing on different industries, or by investing in one mutual fund that contains stock in a variety of industries. Alternatively, you could invest in a number of specific stocks from different industries. Either way, the more industries you diversify across, the less risk you have that one event will affect them all at the same time.

3. Diversify across countries

It makes sense not to invest in only one country's companies. As you may be aware, the Canadian stock market, and the Canadian economy in general, has been lagging behind the American economy for some time now. Furthermore, the Canadian stock market comprises less than five percent of the total value of all of the world's stock markets. In other words, over 95 percent of the total stock market investment available in the world is sold through other countries' stock markets.

As an investor, you probably don't want all of your wealth tied solely to the Canadian economy; instead, you may prefer to diversify across countries and invest some of your money in investments that are issued by companies or governments in other countries.

Outside your RRSP you can invest as much of your money as you want in non-Canadian investments. Inside your RRSP you are allowed to invest up to 20 percent of your total portfolio in non-Canadian investments. Most investment experts recommend that you take advantage of this rule in order to avoid having all of your investments directly tied to the Canadian economy. You can also increase the effective level of non-Canadian investment in your RRSP by picking some mutual funds that qualify as Canadian content but that invest up to 20 percent of their holdings outside of Canada. If you take advantage of these two options, you can increase the non-Canadian content in your RRSP to close to 40 percent. If you really want to avoid the Canadian stock market, you can buy mutual funds that use complex derivative products to mimic the American Dow Jones Industrial Average, the S & P 500 or some other U.S. index. Without breaking RRSP Canadian content rules you will earn the same return as does the U.S. index (minus fund fees).

Another way to reduce your exposure to the Canadian economy is to invest in Canadian companies that sell a large portion of their product outside of Canada. That way their sales and overall financial performance is linked to their product demand outside of the country and is less likely to be affected by a Canadian market downturn. Of course, these companies are exposed to the risks of the economies of the countries to which they export. During the summer of 1998, for instance, as Asian economies faltered, we witnessed the drop in the value of many Canadian companies that exported to Asia.

If you choose to make some of your investments in non-Canadian assets, you do need to keep in mind that some countries are more risky than others. In other words, in the high-risk countries you may make extremely high returns and even double your money in a year or two. On the other hand, you may just as quickly lose half or more of your original investment. Generally, the North American and Western European countries are seen as the least volatile, whereas the emerging markets, such as Latin America, Eastern Europe and Asia are seen as the most volatile and, therefore, as a bigger gamble.

Also, what you choose to invest in, in any country, will influence the overall risk level of your portfolio. Investing in a small Mexican software company, for instance, is much riskier than investing in a large Mexican telephone company. If you are a novice investor, I suggest you stick to U.S. and Western European country diversification.

How Much Diversification Is Enough?

All of this may leave you wondering how much diversification is enough. Generally, the amount of expected volatility in your portfolio is reduced by a decreasing amount with every new type of investment asset you add to it. In other words, the biggest improvement in terms of reducing risk occurs when you go from holding one asset to holding two. Dividing your portfolio into three different investment types further reduces the overall risk but not by as much as does the move from one to two investment types, and so on. After you get to around 10 different items in your investment portfolio, the risk reduction from further splitting is negligible.

The simplest way to become reasonably diversified is to invest in mutual funds. Mutual funds always own at least 10 different underlying assets, so they are diversified by definition. As long as you don't put all of your money into a mutual fund that is highly focused on one industry or one specialized area, you should be relatively diversified. If you want to ensure you are covered for all of the types of diversification covered in this section, you could:

- Put some money in lower-risk investments such as three-year or five-year bonds.
- Put some money in a US or Western European equity-based mutual fund.
- Divide the rest of your money between two Canadian equity mutual funds that are managed by different mutual fund companies.

As we will see in the next chapter, all of these assets can be easily purchased through one investment advisor and kept in a single investment account.

In general, buying mutual funds instead of investing in stocks directly is the easiest way to achieve low-cost diversification in your portfolio. If you want to take on the active management of your own stock portfolio, then you may wish to shift out of mutual funds and into individual stocks. Note, though, that you shouldn't decide to move from mutual funds to investing in individual stocks simply because you are fed up with high mutual fund fees. In fact, the commissions you will have to pay to buy and sell as an individual investor will always be higher than the two to three cents per share that institutional investors such as mutual funds pay. The key factor in choosing to invest directly instead of through mutual funds should really be whether or not you believe you can do a better job of selecting your own investments than could a mutual fund manager.

Making It Happen – Determining Your Personal Risk Profile

This exercise will help you to determine your comfort level with investment risk and give you a clear idea of what types of investments your RRSP and non-RRSP financial assets should be invested in.

Generally, investment advisors suggest that you invest in risky assets when you are younger and less risky assets as you near retirement. For instance, one common guideline is as follows: by subtracting your age from 100, you can determine what percentage of your financial assets should be invested in risky assets such as growth mutual funds or common stock.[10] So if you are 30, then, according to this guideline, you should invest at least 70 percent of your RRSP and non-RRSP assets in higher risk assets.

Overall, the main factors that should influence how much risk you are willing to take on in your investments are:

- your age
- how soon you plan to take your money out of your investments
- how much you can afford to lose
- your personal comfort level
- your investment knowledge and experience

The following questionnaire takes into account these factors and provides a recommended investment mix to suit your needs. Keep track of your points as you complete each question. If you have, or plan on having, an RRSP account and a non-RRSP account with different investing objectives, then you may want to run through the questionnaire twice, considering each account separately.

1. My age is:	**Points**	**My Score**
<30	10	
31-40	8	
41-50	6	
51-60	4	
61-70	2	
71+	0	______

2. I plan to take my money out within the following timeframe:

0 – 2	years	0	
2 - 5	years	2	
5 – 10	years	4	
over 10	years	6	______

3. If I invested $10,000, I would be willing to take the risk of ending up with the following amounts five years from now: (Pick one option)

$10,000 - $11,500	0	
$9,000 - $16,100	2	
$7,700 - $20,100	4	
$5,900 - $24,900	8	______

4. If the value of one of my investments falls by 10 percent from one month to the next, I will:

- Sell it now	0	
- Sell if it is still down at year-end	2	
- Keep it but not invest any more in it	4	
- Not change my investment pattern	6	______

5. My income level is:

< $30,000	0	
$30,001 - $50,000	2	
$50,001 - $75,000	4	
> $75,000	6	______

6. I have this much in my financial investment already:

< $10,000	0	
$10,001 - $50,000	2	
$50,000 - $100,000	4	
> $100,000	8	______

TOTAL POINTS ______

SUGGESTED INVESTMENT MIX

Percent of Financial Investments	0 - 10 Points	11 - 18 Points	19 - 26 Points	27 - 34 Points	35 - 44 Points
Low Risk	75 - 100%	20 - 40%	10 - 30%	0 - 10%	
Med. Risk	0 - 25%	30 - 50%	20 - 40%	10 - 35%	0 - 25%
High Risk		20 - 50%	40 - 60%	65 - 90%	75 - 100%
Highest Risk				0 - 10%	0 - 25%

- Low-risk investments include: money market, GICs, government bonds and high-quality corporate bonds maturing in three years or less (or mutual funds containing these types of assets).
- Medium-risk investments include longer-term high-quality bonds, long standing stocks that pay high dividends, income funds and balanced funds.
- High-risk investments include growth-oriented common stock in Canada, the U.S. or Western Europe (or mutual funds containing these types of assets).
- Highest-risk investments include foreign stock outside of the US or Western Europe and penny stock (or mutual funds containing these types of assets).

This investment risk profile is a guideline for you. You may decide to use your risk profile mix as a three-to-five-year mix objective rather than as an immediate requirement, particularly if your current investments are invested in a much different mix or if you have very little experience in investing.

Divide the circles below into the asset mix that you believe is the best one for you to aim for over the next 12 months. Write the percentage you plan to invest in each asset class next to each slice.

RRSP Non-RRSP

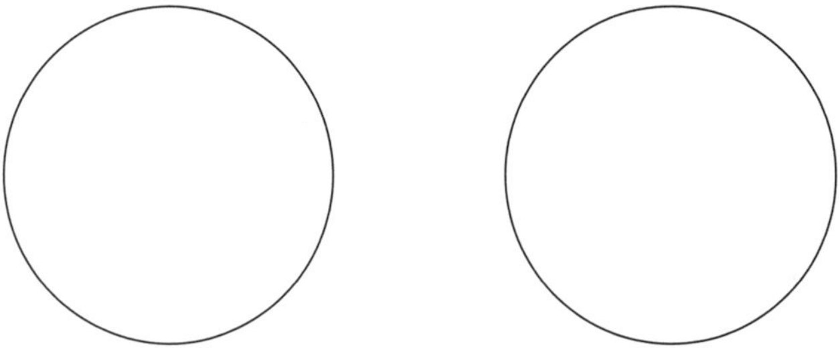

14

Basic Training II

A mighty flame followeth a tiny spark.

DANTE

In the last chapter we covered the importance of diversification and why it makes sense for almost everyone to have some stock in her investment portfolio. Before you get concerned that this all seems awfully complex, let me assure you that all of your financial investments can be managed within one investment account and that any of these investments can be bought or sold with a single phone call. So don't despair: once you get started it can be quite simple. Once we finish reviewing the basic principles of investing, we will move on to how to find the right advisor and start investing.

This chapter contains an overview of how the stock market works and explains three basic systems of investment analysis that are commonly used in selecting investments: technical analysis, fundamental analysis and demographic trend analysis. We will also cover some of the commonly used rules of investing, including dollar-cost averaging and the buy low-sell high rule.

How the Stock Market Works

Although people often refer to the stock market as though it were one central marketplace, there are actually many different stock exchanges set up across North America and around the world. In Canada, the biggest stock exchange is the Toronto Stock Exchange (TSE). The

Montreal, Alberta and Vancouver stock exchanges are smaller, specialized exchanges. In the U.S., the New York Stock Exchange (NYSE) is the biggest exchange.

Not all stock exchanges have the same stocks and financial securities available for trading. When you decide that you want to buy a stock it is not necessary that you know which stock market or stock markets it is listed on. Your investment broker can look that up instantaneously and make the purchase for you. Furthermore, if the security you want is listed on more than one exchange, then it doesn't really matter which exchange you buy on. Whenever a security is listed on more than one exchange, the movement of its price is very similar on all of them.

You may wonder why all stocks are not simply traded on all stock exchanges. This is because each stock exchange has its own set of rules concerning what it will list. A company that wants to have its securities traded on a stock exchange must apply for a listing and meet listing standards for each individual stock exchange in which it is interested. As a result, the large, well-established securities tend to be traded on the largest stock exchanges.

Some securities are not traded on an exchange at all; instead, they are traded "over the counter" (OTC). This means they are traded through a large network of securities brokers and dealers in the National Association of Securities Dealers' Automated Quotation System (NASDAQ). For instance, in the United States, many technology stocks are listed on NASDAQ. Just as your investment advisor can execute a stock trade for you regardless of the stock exchange it is listed on, he or she can also execute any OTC trade you may want. The process, from your perspective, is essentially the same. You call her, tell her what you want to buy or sell and she does it. The transaction is then reported on your next investment account statement.

Investment Strategies – Investment Picking and Market Timing

Basically, all of the fancy investment models and techniques used by investors to make investment decisions boil down to two things: investment picking and market timing. Investment picking refers to selecting specific investments that are likely to increase in value in the future. Market timing refers to predicting when the entire stock market is going to rise or drop and moving your money into or out of stocks in order to take advantage of it.

Most investors focus on investment picking rather than on market timing. This is because market timing is very difficult to do and mistakes can be costly. The market often makes its most significant gains very quickly, and if you miss out on those specific big-gain days, then your stock market returns suffer. For instance, over the 20-year period from the beginning of 1978 to the end of 1997, if you held an initial investment of $1,000 in the TSE 300, then your money would grow to $12,527. If you missed out on the 15 best months of growth, however, you would only have $4,334 at the end of 1997.[1] For most investors, the widely recommended buy-and-hold strategy makes most sense. In other words, buy investments that appear likely to perform well over the long term and hold onto them; do not try to time the market.

With the recent advent of low-cost on-line Internet trading and reduced trading costs, a growing number of personal investors are doing more short-term speculative investing. You may have heard the term "momentum traders," or "day traders," used to describe individuals who place very short-term market timing bets. Often they will invest in one company's stock for less than a day or even for just a few minutes, attempting to capture gains as investor momentum pushes up the stock's price in a short-term burst of demand. Momentum traders base their decisions on investor psychology and the frequent "jump-on-the-band-wagon" behaviour of investors who leap into and out of investments. While some of them make their living from day trading, many rapidly lose their cash. Momentum trading is often compared to gambling, and it is not something on which you want to risk your retirement savings.

Getting back to more sensible investing, how do you decide if an investment has long-term potential? That's where fundamental, technical and demographic analysis come into play. Whether you do it yourself or rely on the recommendations of a full-service investment advisor, this is the type of analysis upon which your investment decisions should be based. Likewise, if you are investing in mutual funds and thereby allowing the mutual fund manager to decide which stocks and securities the fund should hold, then this is the type of analysis she would use.

Fundamental analysis involves examining basic facts about a company and deciding whether or not the value of an investment in it will rise over time. For example, if you were doing fundamental analysis to determine whether to buy stock in Coca-Cola, then you might look at such things as past sales trends and whether the company's strategies make sense. You would consider whether Coca-Cola's management seems capable and stable, what Coca-Cola's major assets are, how well you think Coke can compete with Pepsi and how strong you think the business is overall.

One of the most important measures examined in fundamental analysis is the amount a company currently earns and whether or not earnings are expected to rise in the future. You may have heard of the "P/E ratio." The P/E ratio is the ratio of a company's current total market value (the current stock price multiplied by the total number of shares outstanding) divided by its most recent year's earnings. For instance, if a company's P/E ratio is 40, then this tells you that investors are willing to pay the equivalent of 40 years worth of the past year's profits in order to be owners. They obviously think that the company will be in business for a long time to come and/or that its earnings will grow significantly over time.

Along with other measures, some investors look for companies that have P/E ratios that are lower than they think they should be and then invest in them. The thing to remember with any financial ratio is that it is only one piece of information; to make wise decisions you really need to examine the company in much more depth. For example, if you looked only at P/E ratios, then you would never invest in many of the technology stocks, like Microsoft, that have produced phenomenal returns for investors. This is because the P/E ratio is based on current earnings rather than on future earnings, and these high-tech stocks have grown so quickly that investors have always been willing to pay more than the typical P/E ratio amount.

Another area of information that investors sometimes consider is demographic analysis. Taking demographics into account in, for example, considering Coca-Cola as an investment would entail thinking about which age segments of the population are growing in the countries in which Coca-Cola is sold and whether or not consumers will have the disposable income to buy it. This would help you to predict whether you thought demand for Coca-Cola's product would or would not grow significantly in the future. You would then compare your conclusions about Coca-Cola and its stock against Coca-Cola's market price in order to determine whether or not you thought the stock was undervalued. If you thought it was undervalued, then you would buy stock because you believe that Cola-Cola would outperform other investors' expectations and its price would, therefore, move up over time.

Technical analysis is another form of analysis, but small investors rarely use it. It involves tracking investment price movements and trading volumes using charts and graphs. The idea is that trading patterns can be predicted because they are driven by investor attitudes and psychology. Hence, technical analysts believe that investors can be expected to act in predictable manners when, for example, the stock market index hits the psychological barrier of reaching 10,000. The whole aim of technical analysis is to make short-term bets based more on the anticipated psychological reactions of investors to expected market news than on the underlying value of the company in which you are investing.

You can learn more about fundamental, demographic and technical analyses by reading books that are focused on specific investment techniques or by taking investment courses. My intent in this book, however, is simply to expose you to the terminology and to help you to understand in general terms how investment professionals do the research that enables them to make investment recommendations. My recommendation to you is that you learn by investing first in less risky investments and then, as your understanding grows, in more risky investments. I strongly suggest that, if you are just starting out, you should invest in mutual funds and not directly in stocks. This way a mutual fund manager will be making the specific decisions about which companies the mutual fund should buy and sell, and you only need to decide what type of mutual fund or funds you want to own. In other words, you can decide whether you want a low-risk income fund or a high-risk technology fund, but you can leave the day-to-day investment decisions to the professionals managing the fund.

Even if you want to invest in stocks directly, you should still use a trustworthy full-service investment advisor to provide analysis and to make investment recommendations that suit your needs. If you decide to select your own stocks and bonds, you should still follow the basic investment principles we have covered. Diversifying, matching your investment selections to your risk profile and stock picking rather than market timing all still make sense. However, selecting your own investments basically means that you are choosing to take over the mutual fund manager's job of watching economic and industry developments and deciding where and when you want to place your bets.

Generally, investors shift to self-directed stock investing after gaining investment experience through mutual fund investing, and they begin with industry sectors in which they are well versed. If you work in the telecommunications industry, for instance, you may feel well informed and confident in selecting the specific telecommunications companies that you think will be winners in this rapidly evolving industry. Other approaches include focusing on industry sectors that you believe are going to grow and then researching individual companies within them. This is often the approach of investors who agree with David Foot's demographic-driven demand arguments in *Boom, Bust and Echo*.

Another approach to investment is to focus on companies or industry sectors that, for whatever reason, have fallen out of favour with investors. Warren Buffett, the legendary manager of the Berkshire Hathaway fund, follows this strategy of searching for value buys. Peter Lynch, another industry expert, claims stock returns follow company profit growth, so if you can find companies whose stock price does not reflect the full profit growth you expect from them in the future, then you should invest in them.

Another strategy, and one that I happen to use, involves buying stocks in large, well-known companies that for some reason or other lose a large portion of their share value within a very short timeframe. Nortel Networks is a recent example of this. In 1998 a poor quarterly earnings report drove Nortel's share price down to less than half of what it was at its peak. Less than six months later, it's price had doubled as investor confidence once again returned.

As you can see, there is no one right way to make your investment decisions, and opinions about the best way to invest are almost as numerous as are industry experts. If you decide to take your portfolio solely into your own hands, then you will have to decide which investment strategy to follow.

INDIVIDUAL INVESTOR STRATEGIES

Every investor has her own personal approach to selecting her investments. Clinical psychologist Sandra explains how she has interpreted demographic trends in making her investment decisions: "For me, investing is simply psychology on a larger scale. Demographic trends certainly influence my investing. Demographics are one of the reasons for my computer technology investments. If that industry doesn't grow, then I am sure nothing will."

Sandra has built her $2,000,000 investment portfolio by learning about investing from friends and fellow investors, and she has applied what she knows best – psychology – to predict where she thinks product demand will grow. Clearly, she is willing to take on considerable investment risk – investing in the volatile computer technology industry, for instance – but she hasn't done so blindly. As her investments have grown, so has the amount of time she spends analyzing potential investments. She now reads up to five newspapers a day in addition to considering professional recommendations.

Needless to say, if you choose to invest in individual stocks instead of in funds, you can expect to spend a lot more time doing your own research and making investment decisions. But the good news is that, with the advent of the Internet, individual investors have access to nearly as much information as do the professionals. And for those of us who are so inclined, it can be a very enjoyable pastime.

DOLLAR-COST AVERAGING

In a 1996 Price Waterhouse survey, two of the common responses people gave for not investing in the stock market were: "I don't have enough money to invest" and "Mutual funds are a product for the wealthy."[2] The fact of the matter is that you can start investing in the stock market with as little as $50 or $100 per month by setting up an automatic monthly deposit program through a bank or a stockbroker. This can be an especially good way to begin because it means you do not have to worry about timing your investments. You avoid the fear of making a sporadic major deposit at the wrong time and eliminate this excuse to procrastinate.

By investing the same amount each month, you will actually end up buying more units of stock in months when the price is down and fewer when the price is up. To illustrate, compare a one-time investment of $1,200 versus twelve $100-per-month investments. If you put in $1,200 on January 1, and the value of your investment falls by 10 percent on January 2, you then have $1,080 left. If your investment's value rises by one percent each month for the rest of the year, your investment will be worth $1,216.97 at the end of the year. However, if you only put in $100 on January 1, and another $100 each month following, then your investment will be worth $1,269.66 at the end of the year. You would have earned $52.69 more by spreading out your investment over time and reducing your market timing risk.

With regard to investing directly in bonds rather than in bond funds, many investors use a strategy that involves laddering bonds of varying maturity. For instance, you might construct a five-year "ladder" of bonds by splitting your bond investment funds into five parts and buying five separate bonds that mature in one, two, three, four and five years. Then, as one of the bonds matures each year, you reinvest the proceeds into a new five-year bond. In the end you own five five-year bonds, with one of the five maturing each year and being reinvested at the prevailing five-year interest rate. This way you end up earning the average interest rate over time and avoid sinking all of your money into a single bond that may have a higher or lower interest rate than the long-term average rate.

Consider Your Investments to be a Required Monthly Expense

Many of the women I talked to spoke about "paying yourself first," a phrase you have undoubtedly heard. For most of us who don't have the discipline to save spontaneously, this method works. Setting up a monthly automatic deduction from your paycheque or bank account is the best way for many people to maintain a consistent pattern of investing. Unless you are extremely disciplined, I strongly recommend it.

Debra describes how she feels about her decision to finally get into a regular monthly pattern of saving: "You know, there were many years when I just didn't save. I could kick myself now, because just that $100 per month from when I was 19 and got my first real job, until I was 26 and I finally started investing, would have added up. I would probably have $20,000 more in savings today, maybe more! Most likely, I would have bought a house sooner and I would be further along in paying off my mortgage.

"The best investment decision I ever made was the day I decided that I was going to start. I thought, 'I am really going to do this.' I committed myself to saving, not buying a Canada Savings Bond and cashing it out 12 months later, but saving for the long term.

"What I have found is that if you can get started, you're laughing. Even if it's only $100 a month, it will soon add up. When you look at it a few years later, it's $3,000. That's when you start to feel like you have something of your own. I remember the first day that I realized that I had $5,000 saved. I thought, 'Wow, I finally have something that is mine, which no one can take away from me!' My next thought was, 'Well, how do I get to $10,000 or $20,000?' The larger my net worth grows, the more interesting it gets."

Take Tax Rates into Account

When comparing potential investments take into account the tax rates you will have to pay on your gains. If your investments are held within your RRSP or another tax-sheltered account, then you won't have to pay tax on your gains until you withdraw the money from your account; and all of your withdrawals will be taxed as income. If your investments are not tax-sheltered, then keep in mind that interest returns are fully taxable, whereas dividend and capital gains income are generally taxed at a lower rate (which varies, depending on your province of residence).

Take Calculated Risks, Not Crazy Leaps

The mistaken belief that the stock market is just too complex and risky often results in women being less active in financial markets than men. It also accounts for women beginning to invest at a later age than men. As Connie Roveto of the Bank of Montreal puts it: "There is no mystery. Business is common sense. You have to make more money than you spend. It is the same with personal financial planning. There's no great mystery. As far as I am concerned, there are no great get-rich-quick scenarios. Very few people win lotteries.

"Women can be very competent and very accomplished in terms of their financial security. It is proven over and over again; they just have to become comfortable with the concepts. Basically it comes down to this issue of approach. Men will approach a situation with bravado. It goes back to the schoolyard, where one boy will say, 'I'll jump off this nine-foot fence. Will you?' Women tend to approach things more cautiously. They'll wait until they've researched things and are comfortable. They want to understand the risks involved. They'll ask themselves, 'What is the likelihood of breaking my leg if I jump off the nine-foot fence?' That's the difference. So the financial advice I'd give in terms of achieving the end result is the same whether a client is male or female. But how they approach it, and what they do at different stages, is going to be different for men versus women."

Connie's experience with male and female clients mirrors research findings. Although women are now becoming willing to invest more aggressively, they still lag behind men in terms of the portion of their net worth invested in higher-risk investments, and they still tend to move into these higher-risk investments more slowly over time. There is nothing wrong with this. It is wise to research and understand what you are getting into before you invest. However, fear of complexity or overblown assumptions about the risk involved shouldn't stop you from making equity investments. You owe it to yourself to do the research required to make yourself more comfortable, and you owe it to yourself to take some calculated risks.

Numerous studies actually suggest that, in the long run, patience and planning often make women better investors than men. Overall, women investors have been touted as more diligent researchers, more willing to listen to advice and more likely to stay invested during market fluctuations. This last point is especially pertinent. In a study of 35,000 U.S. households, it was found that men, on average, trade about 77 percent of their investment portfolio each year versus 32 percent for women. This translated into men earning an average of 1.4 percent less in yearly investment returns than did women.3 Women, on the other hand, tended to do more research initially and to focus on buying good-quality stocks and holding them for the long term.4

Connie continues her observations: "I think once women decide to invest they are very diligent in terms of researching either by reading or by meeting with people. They don't want to be talked down to and they don't want to feel that they are asking stupid questions, but they will ask questions. It's like the difference between a woman and a man driving a car trying to get to a destination. The woman will ask for directions along the road, but the man won't. I think it is very similar in terms of their investment behaviour. Men are more likely to base investment decisions more on what their buddies say and so on. Women do their homework and ask for directions from advisors they trust. Of course, these are generalizations and there are lots of exceptions."

Regardless of your level of investment experience, the investment rules covered in this chapter and the last should be kept in mind. Let's review them.

1. Keep it simple, avoid the exotic and complex.
2. Don't lose sleep over your investments. Only invest up to your own risk-tolerance level. Trust your intuition. If your stomach says "No," don't invest.
3. Don't put all of your eggs in one basket. Diversify.
4. Only invest in what you understand. If it doesn't make sense to you, get more information. If it still doesn't make sense, don't invest. Make sure you understand what your maximum potential loss could be before investing. Understand how difficult or easy it will be to get your money out if you need to.
5. Don't buy on tips or rumours. Be skeptical of investment tips on the Internet. Don't speculate. If you want to gamble, then take your money to the casino. It's more fun.
6. Buy and hold.
7. Make investing a monthly habit.

8. Start small, dip your toe in the water before you dive in, but do get wet.
9. Use professional advice, but never abdicate full responsibility for your investment decisions. Stay informed.

Most of all, once you get started, have courage, stick to it and be patient.

15

A Worthy Advisor

No one can make you feel inferior without your consent.

ELEANOR ROOSEVELT

This chapter covers how to find the right investment advisors to work with and how to get the most out of them. But first, let me explain your options concerning where and how you can buy and sell financial assets.

WHO SELLS FINANCIAL PRODUCTS?

Lower-risk savings vehicles can be bought directly through your bank branch. These investments generally pay interest, and your money may be locked-in for a specific amount of time before you can cash in the investment. These investments include guaranteed investment certificates and Canada Savings Bonds.

Furthermore, most major Canadian banks have separate brokerage divisions. These divisions are the same as independent brokerage houses except that a bank owns them. Brokerage houses can buy and sell the same interest-bearing investments as do bank branches, plus a wide range of other investments. Essentially, they can trade any of the stocks, bonds and other financial investments available on any of the Canadian stock exchanges as well as most of the investments available on the U.S. stock markets.

Another option is to work with a financial advisor who is affiliated with a financial advisory company like Investors Group or the Equion

Group. Such advisors generally offer a wide array of various types of investments, including mutual funds and stocks. However, they may not have as broad an offering as the bank brokerage houses, and they may be motivated to steer you towards their own company's investment vehicles. For instance, they may be more inclined to direct you toward mutual funds that their own internal mutual fund managers manage, and not funds managed by other mutual fund companies. Nevertheless, if you are a novice investor, this type of financial advisor can be helpful in defining and refining your entire financial plan, including areas that brokers don't handle, like life insurance.

Another type of investment advisor is the independent financial advisor. She is not directly employed by any specific financial advisory group and, in theory, should be providing unbiased investment advice. However, the difficulty here is that you may have to trade off having someone who is independent and, therefore, relatively unbiased with having direct access to the independent in-house investment research that the full-service brokerages provide for their clients.

Additionally, financial advice and, in some cases, financial advisors can also be found at mutual fund companies and insurance brokerages. However, in Canada, the most popular providers of investment products are independent brokers and dealers as well as banks.[1]

Service, Please

Discount brokers charge lower commissions on most trades than do full-service brokers, but you are expected to do your own investment research and to select your investments on your own. Although discount brokers can sell you a full range of investment products, including stocks, bonds and GICs, and may be able to sell you various research reports, they generally only execute your trades and do not advise you on your decisions. Furthermore, you will likely deal with whichever broker answers the phone or happens to be available. You will not have a specific broker or advisor assigned to you.

Full-service brokers will typically have access to research staff and be able to provide you with ongoing industry and company research reports. Moreover, you can expect them to spend time getting to know your financial goals and interests. They should also, from time to time, alert you to interesting investments within your areas of interest.

Financial advisors will typically play a broader role in your financial affairs than will discount or full-service brokers, and they should be able to provide a wide range of financial advice. Their services are likely to include investment, retirement, estate and tax planning as well as brokerage services.

Last, although I don't recommend it, you can now also trade stock yourself on the same virtual trading floor as do the professionals, using specialized electronic trading room services such as those offered by Swift Trade Securities Inc. You still have to pay trading commissions, but you are able to ensure that your trades are executed immediately rather than being delayed by one of the above intermediaries. For a day trader this is very important, for the rest of us it isn't. And the minimum investment required to gain access to the system makes its cost prohibitive for most investors.

My, What a Big Degree You Have!

There aren't any required credentials for financial planners in Canada, outside of Quebec. Anyone who wants to can call herself a financial planner. However, there are numerous official accreditations to look for.[2]

- A chartered accountant (CA) has extensive training in tax and a broad array of financial matters. She has passed the requirements of her provincial institute of chartered accountants. Training includes years of articling at an accounting firm, extensive accounting courses and exams.
- A certified general accountant (CGA) is trained in corporate accounting and management and is required to meet provincial association requirements.
- A certified management accountant (CMA) has business accounting, management training and provincial association accreditation.
- A certified financial planner (CFP) has personal financial planning training, including at least two years experience. She must also complete 30 hours of continuing education each year in order to maintain her designation.
- A personal financial planner (PFP) is the banking industry's equivalent of a CFP.
- A registered financial planner (RFP) has a CFP and has passed additional courses.
- A chartered financial consultant (CHFC) has passed advanced courses on

financial planning offered by the Canadian Association of Insurance and Financial Advisors (CAIFA).
- A chartered life underwriter (CLU) has written CAIFA exams in order to become a life insurance agent.
- A chartered financial analyst (CFA) has passed exams overseen by the U.S. based Association for Investment Management and Research. Institutional portfolio managers, analysts and investment industry professionals often hold this designation.

To actually sell financial securities, an advisor must also be an investment advisor (IA), an investment counsellor (IC) or an investment representative (IR).

- An IA must pass the Canadian Securities Course in order to be licensed to sell securities.
- An IC is licensed to invest and manage money on behalf of institutions and high-net-worth individuals.
- An IR is licensed to buy and sell securities but not to give investment advice to the public.

Generally speaking, if you are looking for financial investment advice, then you should select someone with specialized training, preferably a CFP, PFP or RFP. If you have a portfolio worth over $150,000, then you may prefer someone with a CFA designation.

Choose Your Advisor with Care

All of the major banks now have brokerage arms, and you can get all of the information on setting up an account at your local branch. Alternatively, you can look in the phone book under Investment Advisory Services or Stocks and Bonds. However, I believe the best way to find a broker is through a personal reference from someone you know.

When Jane started her own consulting business at age 43, she used the Yellow Pages in her search for a financial advisor. "I figured I needed a financial advisor, an accountant and a lawyer. I looked in the phone book. I wanted an accounting firm that was successful, that was making money and that was relatively well known. I wanted a lawyer who was just starting out because I thought that would make them cheaper. And I wanted a financial advisor who was successful too.

"I met the financial advisor and really liked him because he dropped a wine glass. It showed that he was human. It was important to me that the financial advisor and accountant knew each other and also that they were younger than I was, because I don't want them to die when I'm 50. I would have preferred women, but there weren't any that fit the bill. So I picked these two guys who were young, bright and a little bit arrogant. I found a female lawyer.

"The financial advisor is the one that I have the closest relationship with because he needs to know enough about me, my lifestyle and my financial priorities to make informed decisions for me. I am very busy, and as long as my investments are making money over the long run I don't worry about it. As long as they make reasonable returns over six or seven years I don't care about short-term fluctuations. I make decisions based on financial criteria and on my personal values. I figure it is my money so I can do what I want with it, but I don't want to have to nurture my investments and study the pieces of paper. I'd rather pay my advisor to do that."

Given Jane's lack of interest in following her investment closely or doing in-depth research on her own, it makes sense for her to work with a full-service advisor. He makes investment suggestions based on his understanding of her values, investment objectives and tolerance for risk. Jane makes the final call as to whether or not she will buy his recommended investments. Moreover, Jane is not interested in undertaking any market-timing efforts; she is a buy-and-hold, long-term investor. As such, her advisor focuses his recommendations on investments that are expected to grow over the long run rather than suggesting short-term strategies. This is a common approach and is followed by most small investors and most investment advisors.

Nora, a 32-year-old medical sales representative, also shopped around when she was selecting an advisor. "I have two financial advisors. To find them I interviewed about six candidates. I picked these two because they have both been in business for a long time, had good word-of-mouth referrals, seemed concerned about my needs and promised to follow up on a regular basis. They both represent different investment funds, have different areas of expertise and are willing to work together to provide me with the diversification I want. They both know my whole financial position. They need to know my full financial picture to meet my needs well, and the only way I'm willing to share my whole picture is if I know they care about my needs."

Nora is a little unusual in that she works with more than one advisor. However, she also has fairly substantial assets, with a net financial portfolio worth over $100,000, at a relatively young age. It is probably for this reason that her advisors are willing to work together to meet her needs.

Personally, I also work with two different investment accounts, although the difference for me is that only one is with a full-service broker. I invest in his account if he provides me with a specific investment recommendation that I decide to follow. The other account is a discount brokerage account with my bank. I use that investment account to make investments that I have personally researched and decided on without my full-service broker's input. I pay an average of $85 per trade through my full-service broker and $30 per trade through my discount brokerage. By using these two accounts, I only pay the higher fees when I get actual investment research and advice from my full-service broker. Depending on the size of your investment holdings and your interest in doing your own investment research, you may also wish to do this. However, if you are just starting out, or if you are unfamiliar with making investment decisions by yourself, then I suggest you hire a full-service broker or financial advisor. The amount of investment information, advice and research a good advisor can provide is worth the extra cost of higher trading commissions.

When selecting your investment advisor ask yourself the following questions about each potential candidate.

1. Are you comfortable with their credentials, and do you understand what their training involved?
2. How long have they been financial advisors and what level of returns have their clients earned based on their advice? Their tenure can help you judge whether they have a basic level of competence (the weakest advisors usually get weeded out pretty quickly) and gives you an idea of how many market cycles they have been through. If they have only been in business during the 1990s, then they won't have been really tested in a down, or "bear," market. If

they don't have a very long track record, then be sure you have some other compelling reason to work with them.

3. What size of investment accounts do they want their clients to have? What is the average size of their current client accounts? If their typical client account size is similar to what you plan to have, you're likely to be a better fit than would be the case if this were not so.
4. How many clients do they personally serve? A good financial advisor should be able to handle between 100 and 200 families, depending on the range of services provided. If the number is much higher, you may not be adequately served.
5. How often would you be provided with performance reports on your account, and how often would you see your advisors face-to-face? Most firms provide monthly account statements, assuming there is trading activity to report. Otherwise, reports are often quarterly. How often you expect to see your advisors face-to face is a matter of choice. Personally, once a year is plenty for me, since I prefer to conduct all of my financial business over the phone and by mail. What is more important to me is that my broker calls me at least every few months if he hasn't heard from me.
6. What are the services they provide and the types of investments they can offer? Do they have access to hundreds of different bonds and mutual funds or to a more limited number? Do they sell insurance products and other types of financial products? Personally, I would only work with someone who provided a full range of Canadian and American mutual funds, stocks and bonds.
7. What fees do they charge for each type of service they provide? Look for fees that seem reasonable according to what other advisors charge and according to how much you think the service will benefit you.
8. What is their investment philosophy? Do they make speculative recommendations if clients so desire? Do they stick to clients who have long-term savings goals and want to buy and hold? Do they make market-timing recommendations? How about stock picking? Do they have specialized expertise in one or more areas of investment in which you might be interested (e.g., estate planning)? It is crucial that their investment philosophy matches your own.
9. What do they think your investment portfolio would be likely to contain if they worked with you? Make sure their suggested investments match the level of risk with which you are comfortable.
10. Can they provide references? Call each reference and ask her how happy she/he is with this broker and why.

After you have concluded your initial meetings with the candidates, ask yourself the following questions.

1. Do their typical clients sound like you?
2. Do they have the products and services in which you are most interested?
3. Would you be embarrassed asking them questions or feel intimidated dealing with them?
4. Most important, are you comfortable with them?

Once you think you've found someone who is likely to meet your needs and with whom you feel comfortable, open an investment account with her and make an initial investment. Don't necessarily move all of your savings into this account right away; instead, you may want to test your advisor by opening an account and initially giving her a small amount of money to invest on your behalf.

See how she does. Is she steering you towards investments you feel comfortable with and that make sense to you? Does she provide you with the information you want when you ask? Can you reach her easily at your convenience? Are these investments performing at or ahead of the average for their investment category? In other words, is the balanced mutual fund she suggested performing well compared to all balanced mutual funds? Is the health care sector fund she suggested one of the best health care funds? She should be able to provide you with comparative investment return information. And last, do you feel comfortable with her?

If the answer to all of the above questions is "Yes," then it looks like you've found a winner. If the answer to one or more is "No," then you may wish to shop around some more.

Once you have set up a trading account, you can then make trades whenever you want, usually as easily as placing a phone call to your broker or advisor, mailing in a cheque or placing an order over the Internet.

Fees Aren't Everything

Be aware that there are other fees associated with investing besides brokerage transaction fees. If your advisor gets involved in your overall financial planning, including estate planning, tax planning and/or insurance planning, then there are likely to be separate fees for these services. Also, if you buy mutual funds rather than individual stocks, then the buying-and-selling fees are typically a percentage of the amount you invest rather than a set dollar amount. Mutual fund transaction fees range from nothing (no-load funds) to as high as five percent. Furthermore, you often have the choice of paying these fees when you invest (front-end load) or when you sell (back-end load). The catch with selecting a back-end load is that if you sell within the first few years of owning the mutual fund, then the fee is usually higher than it would have been had you paid the front-end load. Over time, back-end loads usually decline as a reward for keeping your money in that particular fund.

Another fee involved in all mutual funds is the mutual fund manager's yearly management fee. Typically, the management expense ratio (MER) runs between one and two percent of your investment. This means that your real investment return will be one to two percent lower than the overall performance reported by the mutual fund company each year, since the percentage gain or decline in overall fund value is publicly reported without management fees deducted. Nevertheless, I wouldn't get too hung up on fees. While lower fees can mean higher returns for you at the end of the day, I believe very strongly that you should select your investments based on investing your money in the industry sectors in which you are most interested and with mutual fund managers who have good track records. In my opinion, the gains you are likely to make from these two factors outweigh a few percentage points paid in yearly fees. Personally, I generally ignore investment fees as long as they are not out of line with the percentages I mentioned above – a sales fee of one to five percent and a MER under three percent.

Do Your Part

If you are new to financial investing, then I strongly suggest you use some sort of an investment advisor to help guide your stock market moves. At the same time, it is a good idea to familiarize yourself with alternative sources of investment information. This is not a necessity, but it will help you to more fully understand what is happening with your money and allow you to make better-informed decisions about where to invest. Your efforts can involve as little as starting to read *Fortune* magazine once a month.

There is a multitude of investment information available all around you. *The Globe and Mail* provides good overall Canadian business coverage. There are a number of investment newsletters available on the Internet, many of which are free. In major cities, most brokerage houses offer free investment seminars on an ongoing basis. You can watch stock market analysts pontificate on market conditions on TV. You can attend a personal financial management course at your local university. Or you can subscribe to investment letters that provide specific investment recommendations. Whichever way you choose to continually increase your knowledge of investing, the more you know, the more likely it is you will be able to both enjoy and maximize your investments.

Making It Happen -- Selecting a Financial Advisor

This exercise is designed to help you to hire a financial advisor or to re-evaluate your current sources of financial advice.

Finding the right financial advisor is like having the right medical doctor. It takes a little effort, but once you've found someone with whom you are comfortable and with whom you can communicate well, the rewards are significant. While taking good care of your body with the help of a competent physician can lead to a longer life, taking good care of your finances with a competent advisor can help that longer life be much more comfortable.

1. Define the type of advisor you want.

A. What types of investment products are you looking for?

Check if Important	Investment Product
	Basic interest-bearing products (money market, GIC's, T-bills, bonds)
	Mutual Funds
	Stock
	Foreign mutual funds, stocks and bonds
	Insurance products

B. What types of investment services do you want?

Check if Important	Investment Services
	Investment buying and selling
	Investment research reports on specific investments
	Investment recommendations
	Financial planning (investment portfolio advice)
	Tax planning and return completion
	Estate planning
	Other

C. How much money do you expect to have in your account five years from now? $ ______________________

D. What sort of investment philosophy are you comfortable with?

Check if Important	Investment Philosophy
	Long-term buy and hold
	More active investment picking and market timing
	Focus on short-term gains
	Speculative investing
	Other

E. What other characteristics are important in your investment advisor?

____

____

____

2. Develop a list of three to five potential advisors.

Whom will I ask to recommend an advisor? ______________________

- ______________________
- ______________________
- ______________________

Where else will I look for potential advisor names?

- ______________________
- ______________________

I plan to have this step completed by: ______________________

3. Arrange a meeting with each potential advisors.

Potential Advisor Name and Phone #	Meeting Date	Meeting Location and Time

I plan to have this step completed by: ____________________

4. Meet with potential advisors and evaluate fit.

Questions	Answers Candidate #1	Answers Candidate #2	Answers Candidate #3
Training			
Years of Experience			
Typical Client Portfolio Size			
Number of Clients			
Performance Report Frequency			
Face-to-face Frequency			
Services Offered			
Fees - per trade - account fees - advice - other			
Investment Philosophy			
Likely Investment Portfolio for Me			
References and Phone Numbers			

5. Select the advisor that is right for you.

Sizing Up the Fit	Candidate #1	Candidate #2	Candidate #3
Do their typical clients sound like you?			
Do they have the products and services in which you are most interested?			
Would you be embarrassed asking them questions or feel intimidated dealing with them?			
Most important, are you comfortable with this person?			

I have decided to hire: ______________________________

Once you've made this very important decision, keep asking questions, follow your investments and, over time, re-evaluate whether this investment advisor meets your needs. If not, then you always have the right to choose a different advisor, and you now know how to do this.

16

The Roof over Your Head

We poison our lives with fear of burglary and shipwreck and, ask anyone, the house is never burgled and the ship is never wrecked.
JEAN ANOUILH

Real estate is a great investment for many women, either in the form of buying their own home or by investing in revenue property. In this chapter we'll explore both types of purchase.

Ada is 55. She divorced at age 40 and never remarried. An Italian immigrant with a high school education, she has always worked in menial jobs; currently she is a nanny. Nevertheless, Ada owns real estate. She has about $400,000 worth of equity built up in 12 residential rental units.

Ada describes her decision to start investing in real estate: "I only started this about five years ago. When I was younger, raising my children alone, I felt helpless and felt sorry for myself. I never thought about taking control of my life. As I got older, I realized this attitude was stupid, and I decided to start taking better care of myself and not wait for someone else to do it.

"When my eldest son started working, he came to me with the idea of taking equity out of my house to buy a four-plex as a revenue property. We live in Calgary and, at the time, we thought that Calgary real estate prices would go up and we were right. So Gino and I bought the four-plex together, and that's how I got started." None of the initial fears

Ada had about losing money or not being able to find tenants materialized, and a year later she bought a small apartment building with six more units. This was followed by a third building with four more units. The value of her investments has increased by $200,000 since she started.

Ada definitely bought at the right time and in the right place. Her self-confidence has grown immeasurably since she has begun investing, and she feels really good about what she has accomplished.

A Castle of Your Own

If Ada's story sounds attractive to you, then the first question to ask yourself is whether you really want to own real estate. If you do, then the next question is whether you want to own a home to live in yourself or a property that you rent out. Let's start with the scenario of buying your own home.

Owning a home is a big commitment. Not only will you invest a large sum of money in purchasing it, but the cost of maintenance, both in terms of time and money, can be high. At the same time, buying a home usually means no longer paying rent against someone else's mortgage, and it offers lifestyle benefits such as having a yard and decorating as you choose. Home ownership can also provide you with a "forced" monthly investment in the form of your mortgage payment; and your capital gains, when you sell, are tax-free if your home is your principal residence. Furthermore, there are many ways to earn income from your investment while you own it.

Personally, I consider a home to be one of the most enjoyable and sensible investments you can make. That is, of course, if the home ownership lifestyle is appealing to you and if you make your purchase decision on the basis of careful analysis of the property's investment potential and resale value rather than on the basis of emotion.

The Case for Starting Modestly

Before you take the plunge, you need to determine what you can afford. A common rule is to ensure that your monthly housing costs do not exceed 32 percent of your gross monthly income. Monthly housing costs include monthly mortgage principal and interest, property tax and heating as well as half of any monthly condominium fees. The other commonly used affordability rule is: your entire monthly debt load should not be more than 40 percent of your gross monthly income.

However, just because you can afford this much doesn't mean you should spend this much. Keep in mind that in addition to mortgage payments, property tax, utilities and condominium fees, you may also face repair bills, renovation and decorating costs. Be sure to take this into account when determining your anticipated post-purchase monthly budget. Be careful not to get carried away with the glamour of a big expensive home. Getting in over your head will only do two things: keep you up at night worrying about bills and ensure that you pay too much in mortgage interest.

Consider this scenario. You have a $25,000 down payment saved up. You have an eight percent mortgage, and you plan to pay $1,000 per month against your mortgage until your home is paid off. You have a choice of buying a $150,000 home now or buying a $100,000 starter home and trading up to a $150,000 home once the first house is paid off.

If you buy the $150,000 home now, then it will take you roughly 22 years to pay off your mortgage, and you will have paid more than $140,000 in interest over and above the actual $150,000 purchase cost of your house.

If you bought a $100,000 starter home, then it would be paid off in less than nine years and you could avoid spending over $1,000 on the mortgage insurance that is required when you make a down payment of less than 25 percent of the total purchase price. Assume the market stayed flat and you then sold your first house, incurring $7,000 in real estate fees, and bought the $150,000 home. Your second home would be paid off six years later. In total, you would have paid only $50,000 in interest and real estate fees. Plus, you would be mortgage-free seven years faster! You end up spending a lot less on interest by starting out more modestly.

Ellen and her husband followed the start-modestly-and-then-trade-up scenario. "One of our strategies to save for a house when we first got married was to do without anything that we could do without. If we knew that we could get by for the next day or week or month or year without it then we did without it. Even things like not buying garbage cans when plastic bags would do. You had to keep your eye on the prize because there are a lot of things along the way that can really push you off that path."

By paying off their first house in four years and then trading up, Ellen and Jim have minimized their interest expenses. Their new house is almost paid off, and now they have many years of mortgage-free living ahead of them.

Of course, you don't want to be trading up continually. Unlike investments in stocks and bonds, where the decision to sell an investment costs as little as $25 in sales commission, real estate agent fees can be substantial. While the buyer doesn't pay any sales commission, the seller typically pays seven percent of the first $100,000 in home value and three percent of the remainder. In other words, if you sell a house for $150,000, then your real estate fees total $8,500. So buying and selling more often than every five years should be avoided.

Okay, But How Can I Afford It?

Don't be discouraged if home ownership looks too expensive for you. There are many ways you can reduce home ownership costs and still enjoy your own home. Two common methods involve renting out basement suites and garages. For instance, Louise, who raised three children single-handedly on a librarian's salary, has always used these revenue sources to make ends meet. Although you have to claim your rental income on your tax return, you can deduct many maintenance and repair expenses against this income. When shopping, just let your real-estate agent know you are looking for a home with a legal basement suite or a home zoned for multiple occupancy with a basement that can be easily developed into a suite.

Other alternatives include having a roommate, doing your own repairs and delaying renovations. Jennifer has purchased older homes, the first when she was 26, and renovated them herself. Although her real estate investments haven't always worked out perfectly, she has enjoyed them and continues to own her own home. "I have a fascination with homes and renovating. My first home, in 1989, was a fixer-upper that only cost $53,000. It had a great location near the university, hardwood floors, hot water radiators and a suite in the basement. It was orange and purple and had never been updated, but it was a good investment.

"I did most of the renovating work with the help of my brother. I put in new drywall and new cupboards in the kitchen. In the basement I installed a new countertop and cupboards. I painted, refinished the hardwood and added new bedroom carpet. I put very little money into it; it was mostly elbow grease.

"Having someone in the basement suite was nice, too. If you live alone and travel a lot like I did, it's good to have someone in the house. Plus, after rental income, I only had to pay utilities and $100 a month towards my mortgage to live there, even though I had only put 10 percent down."

Jennifer moved out of town in 1993 and sold her house for $65,000, making it a profitable investment.

Finding the Money

You can purchase your first home with a down payment as small as five percent of the total purchase price of your home. Moreover, if you are a first-time buyer, the Canadian government allows you to withdraw up to $20,000 from your RRSP for a down payment. If you are buying a home with another first-time buyer, you are both eligible to withdraw up to $20,000. You must then repay the money taken out of your RRSP over the next 17 years, but you are not required to make any repayments within the first two years. After that you need to repay at least one-fifteenth per year.[1]

If you can afford to put down 25 percent or more, you will save the cost of mortgage insurance. Mortgage insurance protects the mortgage lender against the risk of you defaulting on your mortgage. A higher down payment can also help you sleep better at night, knowing you are not over-financed.

Regardless of the size of your down payment, you will most likely have to borrow money to buy. Banks, trust companies, credit unions, caisses populaires in Quebec and finance companies are all potential mortgage lenders, so you can shop around. All institutes give discounts on the published mortgage rate to attract clients, so decide what type of mortgage you want and ask for their best offer.

In selecting a mortgage you need to decide what term you want, whether you want a fixed-rate or variable-rate mortgage and any special features you may want. The term determines how long you and the lender are committed to the mortgage. At the end of the term, your mortgage comes up for renewal and is renegotiated.

Whether you select a fixed-rate mortgage with a locked-in interest rate or a variable-rate mortgage with a floating interest rate depends mostly on your tolerance of uncertainty. A variable-rate mortgage means your mortgage payment will fluctuate depending on changes in interest rates. Most people opt for a fixed-rate mortgage.

Furthermore, once you have decided what type of mortgage you want, consider special features, such as the opportunity to make extra yearly lump-sum payments against your mortgage, or the option to make double payments on occasion. These features can help you break a tie between two lenders offering the same interest rate. Last, don't wait until you've found a home you want to buy before securing a mortgage. Get pre-approved before you house hunt. This way you'll know how much you have to spend and won't be scrambling at the last minute.

Deciding What You Want

Before you go shopping you should give some thought to your purchase priorities. It's usually impossible to find a property with everything you want, so knowing what's important and what you can compromise on makes the search easier. Things you can't change – like location, proximity to services that are important to you and proximity to work – are often at the top of buyers' lists.

In your mind, try to flesh out a picture of what you are looking for, but be flexible. Giving a lot of thought to what you are looking for early on means that you will be less susceptible to "falling in love" with a house and making a highly emotional choice rather than a balanced, rational one.

A Real Estate Agent You Trust

Just as finding an investment advisor you trust is important, so is finding a real estate agent you trust. Key considerations include their knowledge and experience in the field and in the neighbourhoods that interest you, how comfortable you feel with them and your sense that they understand what you want and will do whatever it takes for you to be satisfied. Recommendations from friends, colleagues and relatives are extremely helpful with regard to finding prospective agents. Or you can visit open houses and talk to the hosting agent, or you can look in the phone book. Regardless of how you find potential agents, you should always interview them to ensure compatibility before you agree to work with them.

DON'T BE PENNY-WISE AND POUND-FOOLISH

When you've found a property you like, you should always have it inspected to uncover any hidden flaws. Make your offer to purchase conditional on receiving a satisfactory home inspection report and invest a few hundred dollars in peace of mind.

BECOMING A LANDLORD

If you are considering investing in a revenue property, then there are some additional factors to consider. Most important, you need to make sure you are comfortable with making a substantial investment that requires a multi-year commitment and that is costly to exit. If you want to minimize these factors but still place a bet on real estate, then you may wish to invest indirectly in a Real Estate Investment Trust (REIT) through your broker.

When buying a revenue property, you really need to make sure that the numbers add up. This is not the time to let emotion take over. Estimating your return on investment (ROI) and understanding the potential risks that may affect it, before you buy, is crucial. To do this, use the following formula: Yearly ROI = [Yearly revenue – expenses + mortgage principal paid off per year + estimated yearly increase in resale value] ÷ amount invested. Generally, your yearly revenue equals all of your rental income. Take into account any potential vacancy time based on vacancy rates in the city, any seasonal vacancies that may occur if you rent to students and any time you will need to keep the space empty to do renovations. Your yearly expenses include mortgage payments, property taxes, utilities, maintenance, renovations and the cost of a property manager (if you use one). Your mortgage lender can supply the amount of mortgage principal that would be paid down each year and, to be conservative, I would suggest you assume that there is no yearly increase in resale value. The ROI you calculate is before tax, since the gains on the sale of a revenue property are taxable. If you are happy with the estimated return and comfortable with the risk, then being a landlord may be for you.

Treat Real Estate like Any Other Investment

Regardless of the expense and risk involved, many of the women I interviewed for this book had invested in real estate. It seems to be an investment many women can relate to and one in which we can find personal fulfillment. If you make investing in your own home a primary component of your personal financial plan, then I think it is very likely that you will get a great deal of joy from your investment while its value grows.

The key thing in this investment, as in any other, is to do your homework and then listen to your gut. If you don't feel comfortable, then stop, figure out what is causing your concern and proceed only after you have resolved the issue. If it is more research that you need to do, then do more research. If you need to lower the price range you are considering, then do that. If you need to trade in your real estate agent for one you feel more comfortable with, then go ahead. This is likely to be one of the biggest investments you will ever make. You owe it to yourself to take as much time and use as much caution as you desire. In the end, you'll be glad you did.

In the meantime, consider Diane's success. At age 33 Diane has a net worth of $220,000. Her wealth is the product of her using savings from her income as a sales representative to make shrewd real estate investments. Diane is able to make up to a 25 percent return on her investment each year by carefully selecting the properties she buys. Here is her story. "My father bought revenue properties while I was growing up. I remember him taking real estate courses and that sort of thing. Also, my older brother has been quite successful investing in real estate. So they influenced me to buy real estate. I watched their progress and I knew that when I had money I wanted to do the same.

"I bought my first revenue property seven years ago in Saskatoon. I was 26. At that point in my life I had a boyfriend and I wanted to get married. He was moving out of one house and into another house. I thought that would be a good opportunity for us to begin bringing our lives together, but he wasn't game, so I bought my own house. Rather than sitting around and moping about it, I just got on with my life and made my own investment decision. I didn't have quite enough for a down payment, but I got a line of credit and used some of it towards my down payment. The revenue that the house generated each month was enough for me to pay for the mortgage, repairs and payments against my line of credit. It has been great. I love the house, it's beautiful. It's a character home and no problem to rent. I still have the house, although I no longer have the boyfriend.

"I've bought additional places since then. The next place that I bought was a condominium in Saskatoon, about a year later. Every time I've bought a property I have never had quite enough money for the down payment so I've always done a bit of creative financing. In this case the seller was asking for about $35,000, so I offered $31,000 and asked for a $2,000 decorator bonus. This way I got $2,000 up front and used it as part of my down payment.

"When I buy a place I always look at what my return will be on the money that I put down. The condominium generated about $550 per month in rent. The condominium fees were $90 per month and the mortgage payment was about $200. For the most part the condominium association did the repairs, and the condominium fee had a large contingency fund for repairs. So I was making about $200 per month on my original investment of $6,000 – a 40 percent return on investment.

"A couple of years after the condominium I bought a triplex and a duplex with my brother in Winnipeg. Each year after that I bought one more property. Last year my brother and I bought an 11-suite apartment.

"When I'm shopping for a new investment I just go and look at places. The first thing is that gut feeling, like, 'This is great, this is beautiful, this place is in such great condition.' I look for something that I'd like to rent myself. I look and look and look. Then after I get this feeling of 'Wow,' I do the numbers and agonize a bit.

"Of course, over time I've had problems with tenants not paying their rent and so on. To me it's just part of the business. I have a property manager in both cities, and for five percent of the revenue they look after all of the tenant interaction and accounting. I look at the property manager as sort of an employee. I think of it as good management experience for me. I'm learning how to follow up with her and make sure she does what she says she is going to do.

"Although you might think I have a high tolerance for risk, I don't think of it as risk. The revenue is there to support the debt. I plan for the major repairs that will need to be done, it's just part of keeping the place in good condition. I reinvest some of my profit and write that off against the revenue. I don't see it as a big risk.

"I used to invest in the stock market too, but I lost some money there. I found that it wasn't as real or as interesting either. With stocks I don't have any control. They are a big company and I don't know what they are going to do. If their stock goes down, how do I get it to go back up? What am I going to do? But if something goes wrong with a house, well, I can go out and get some price quotes and get it fixed.

"I did have a few stressful moments when there were floods in Winnipeg because there is no flood insurance for any homes in Winnipeg. But if you have a job and you have to get a proposal in, there is stress involved. Or if you're a salesperson and you are waiting for a big order, that's stressful too.

"I don't want to get all of my money solely from my job. I ended up getting fired from a job a few years ago. Financially I could have quit, but I was too determined to make it work. I couldn't accept failure at that point because it was such a mundane, stupid job. My properties are my insurance policy in life. If anything goes wrong with a job, I can still be self-sufficient."

Diane feels that she has more control over her tangible real estate investment than she would have over financial investments – a feeling shared by many other women. I can understand why: homes are something a lot of women have experience caring for. Domestic details like utility bills and window coverings are familiar, whereas many of us have no direct experience with dividends, stock splits and P/E ratios.

Some women feel more comfortable with real estate and are, therefore, able to make an investment in this arena with little anxiety.

Diane's real estate investing is aggressive compared to that of most people, but her story conveys some important points. First, she's been able to do it on her own – no husband, no second income, no gifts from mom and dad. Second, she listens to her intuition but is also very practical in her approach. Third, she's doing something she enjoys and understands, so it's not overly stressful for her. She believes she will do well and that everything will work out fine, and it does. You can choose to do this too, if you like. Whether it's a small home of your own or a large revenue property, if you take a careful approach to it and work within your means, there is no reason real estate can't be a successful investment for you too.

Making It Happen – Researching Real Estate

1. Gather information.

For the novice, a good place to start is at a local home-buying seminar. A good seminar should be free and should include presentations by real estate agents, mortgage lenders, real estate lawyers, home inspectors and other home purchase professionals. Attending does not oblige you to buy anything. Another good place to get information is in your local Canada Mortgage and Housing Corporation (CMHC) Office. This government organization's goal is: "Helping to house Canadians." CMHC offers a wide range of housing-related information and publishes The Complete Guide to Buying Your Home. This is a step-by-step workbook that takes you through each step of the home purchase process.

Steps I plan to take to gather information:

- ________________________________
- ________________________________
- ________________________________
- ________________________________
- ________________________________
- ________________________________
- ________________________________
- ________________________________
- ________________________________
- ________________________________

2. Figure out what you can afford.

Review your net worth statement from Chapter 6 and evaluate how much of a down payment you can afford. Familiarize yourself with current mortgage rates and begin the pre-approval process with at least one potential lender. Pre-approval is free and does not oblige you to buy anything.

Steps I plan to take to figure out what I can afford:

- ________________
- ________________
- ________________
- ________________

3. Decide what you want.

Make a list of critical and non-critical features. Prioritize the list, giving higher priority to things about which you are not willing to compromise and lower priority to things about which you are flexible. Investigate whether what you are looking for is within your price range by checking the newspaper, Internet and library resources. If you can't afford what you want, then either adjust your requirements or continue saving.

Steps I plan to take to decide what I want:

- ________________
- ________________
- ________________
- ________________

4. Find a good agent and start looking.

With regard to finding a real estate agent, use the same sort of process that is described in Chapter 15 with regard to finding a financial advisor. Decide what you are looking for in an agent, interview potential candidates and select one with whom you are comfortable.

Steps I plan to take to start shopping:

- ________________
- ________________
- ________________
- ________________

17

Completing the Puzzle

The time to repair the roof is when the sun is shining.

JOHN F. KENNEDY

THE MOMENT OF TRUTH

At this point, we've covered a lot of ground. This is the moment of truth. You now understand more about what you are doing financially and why you do it, and you are working to enhance your financial attitudes. Now it is time to pull all of the numbers together into a personal financial action plan, taking into account your goals, your current financial situation, your budget and your risk profile. So sharpen your pencil!

You have assessed your current situation and developed personal and financial goals for the next five years and the next 20 years. But between your RRSP account, your short-term savings objectives and the debt you may owe, you still may not be clear on exactly where to put your monthly savings first.

ERADICATE YOUR DEBT

Well, unfortunately, the first step is probably the least exciting. Pay off your debt. Debt is paid off using after-tax money while investment profits are usually taxable. You need to earn investment returns that are a lot higher than your debt interest rates in order to come out ahead by investing rather than paying off debt.

Let me illustrate. Assume your credit card charges 14 percent per year on outstanding balances. Assume you are in the 50 percent marginal tax bracket. In other words, at your income level, for every additional dollar you earn you pay 50 percent to the government in tax. In this instance, if you chose to invest $1,000 for a year instead of using it to pay down your credit card debt, then you would have to earn over 28 percent on your investment to come out ahead. A 28 percent return on $1,000 is $280. After paying 50 percent tax you would be left with $140. Meanwhile, your $1,000 credit card debt would have cost you $140 in interest. So in the end you just break even. Earning a 28 percent annual return is a rare event; since its inception, the Canadian stock market has only averaged about 10 percent.

The first step in improving your financial position is always paying down your debt. Start with whatever charges the highest interest rate. Pay that down first. When you have no debt left except for a home mortgage, you can then focus on building your investments.

The only exception to this rule is if you know that you just don't have the stamina to be this disciplined. If you know that you will only be motivated to continue with your plan by building a financial nest egg and watching it grow, you may prefer to work hard at paying down your debt while, at the same time, building your savings. You will pay more debt interest than you should, but if it keeps you motivated it is worthwhile.

In the meantime, keep a strong focus on changing your debt beliefs. Use your affirmations. Picture the debt leaving your life. In your mind's eye, pile your debt in a garbage bag in front of your house and have a large bird carry it off into the sky. Concentrate on how it will feel when your debt is gone. Can you feel the weight lifting? Let go of your debt and focus on the peacefulness of healthy financial living.

Protect Your Investments from Revenue Canada

As you enact your plan, take advantage of your RRSP. If you have unused room left in your RRSP and you earn enough income to pay tax, then you should make your financial investments inside of your RRSP. This doesn't mean that your money will be locked in until you retire. It just means that when you take money out of your RRSP you have to pay tax on your withdrawal, since it is considered to be part of your income that year. For some people a good time to take money out of RRSPs occurs when they return to school after working. Putting money in during high tax bracket years and taking it out during low tax bracket years can be a good idea, just as long as you are still building your net worth in some other way.

If you have children, then you may also wish to save for their education within a tax-sheltered Registered Education Savings Plan (RESP). Unlike an RRSP, there is no tax deduction for contributions, but the investment earnings within the RESP are not taxable until withdrawn. Furthermore, the government will match 20 percent of your contribution to a maximum of $400 per child, per year. In other words, if you contribute $2,000 to an RESP for your child, then the government will add $400. When your children withdraw the money, they are only taxed on the investment gains, and if they are like most students, then they will have such low income that their tax bracket will be negligible. Moreover, should your child choose not to attend a post-secondary institute, you can still get your initial investment out, although you will be required to pay a financial penalty.

Save Toward Your Goals

Beyond debt repayment, RRSP and RESP priorities, deciding where to direct your remaining savings is up to you. Personally, I believe that buying your own home is a wise investment choice. However, your life priorities may not include home ownership. Your priority may be saving to travel for a year or buying a vacation home. The choice is yours, just as long as you are saving for something.

Making It Happen – Finalizing Your Personal Financial Plan

This exercise is crucial, so please give it your full attention. Also, I suggest you use a pencil, since it is very likely that you will make changes along the way.

Start by reviewing your personal and financial goals from Chapter 5. Are they in sync? Is there anything you want to adjust? Once you are happy with your longer-term goals, translate them into shorter-term financial goals in the chart below. State what your goal is in each financial category and how much money it will require each month.

Then go back to your budget in Chapter 7. How much money do you have each month as net monthly savings? Copy that number into the chart. Do your net monthly savings cover your investment requirements? If not, then make adjustments in your budget and goals until both numbers match and you are satisfied with your savings level.

Financial Goal Area	**My Twelve-month Goals**	**Monthly Amount**
Debt Reduction - Credit card debt reduction - Loan repayment - Other		
Retirement - RRSP contribution		
Short-term Goals - Housing (down payment or extra mortgage payments) - Major household expense (car, trip, etc.) - Education - Other		
Other Investment Goals		
Total Investment Needs	Add monthly requirements above	$
Net Monthly Savings	From your budget in Chapter 7	$
Difference		$

Now list the remaining steps you need to take in order to put your plan into action. They might include hiring a financial advisor or setting up investment accounts and automatic monthly investment deductions. They may include cancelling your cable to save money or selling your second car. They may include asking for a raise or moving some of your existing investments to different risk categories to match your personal risk profile. They might include writing down your positive money affirmations 25 times each morning and night.

Whatever you need to do, list below.

Steps I Need to take to Put My Plan into Action	Anticipated Completion Date
1.	
2.	
3.	
4.	
5.	
6.	
7.	
8.	

There you go. Your action plan is complete. You know what to do and you know how to do it. You understand more about bringing financial security and balance into your life than most people. All you have to do is choose to continue moving forward. So complete the steps you've listed above and turn your new behaviour into enjoyable habits.

As you continue down the path, monitor your progress. Review your plan at least once a year to make sure you are on track and to make adjustments as your life evolves. During the next 12 months reassess your progress frequently, especially if the lifestyle adjustments you need to make to meet your plan are significant. A monthly check-up, until you are satisfied that you are on course, makes sense.

Don't be discouraged if you don't achieve everything you want to immediately. Any step forward is a step in the right direction, and you've already taken the most important step of all – developing the right mental attitude. As you change your mind, you change your life. What you believe, you achieve; and the more you change, the easier change becomes. So celebrate your successes, forget your failures and keep moving ahead. You'll be glad you did.

18

Taking Care of Yourself for Life

Who ever walked behind anyone to freedom? If we can't go hand in hand, I don't want to go.

HAZEL SCOTT

We have now come to the final element of the prosperity equation – protecting your wealth. Here we will cover the essential elements involved in protecting your financial security, including maintaining involvement in your own financial future regardless of your relationship status, insuring your most precious assets (including yourself) and always maintaining a will. We'll delve into various women's financial experiences in and out of relationships and explain how you can protect your financial health and bolster your relationship at the same time. Let's start by talking about why protection is so important in the first place.

Let's face it, for the vast majority of women, financial success is secondary to relationship success. There is nothing necessarily wrong with this. Frankly, I applaud our dedication to relationships; they are an essential element in a meaningful life. However, too often we disregard our finances for fear that respecting and protecting our money will harm our marriage prospects. You might think this doesn't apply to you. Well, have you ever left a job for a relationship? Moved for a relationship? Given up a promotion? Not made an investment, such as buying a home, because you were waiting until after you got married? Ignored your financial future because you had a husband to take care of you? If so, then the lessons in this chapter may apply to you more than you realize.

In a healthy union, having both partners involved in the finances is beneficial. This doesn't mean you have to balance the chequebook together, but you should have shared financial goals and you should both be up to date on the state of your joint financial welfare.

The Monster under the Bed May be just a Shadow

Although many women are taking more responsibility for their own financial well-being, I have yet to come across a woman for whom the adjustment from traditional "man-as-breadwinner-and-asset-owner" bias has been without some angst. Overcoming the assumptions that his career always comes first, his RRSP is more important and it is okay if he is the only one contributing to a pension plan is a scary, but liberating, process for many women. Below, Cecily, a 57-year-old retired nurse, talks about overcoming her fear of money matters and her own mother's struggle with the topic.

"My father was a machinist. My mother was a housewife until all four children left home. My childhood modelling was that the woman stayed home and the father had most of the power and certainly all of the money.

"When my mother was in her forties she went back to work, first as a cleaning woman and then in a hospital kitchen. Later she took a course and became an EKG technician. Watching her start to pay into a pension for herself, even though she started late, has had a big impact on me.

"Some years later, after my dad died, she would visit me and we would talk about everything from soup to nuts. Every time we talked about money she would be in tears. She couldn't talk about money at all. I'd sit there and say, 'Mom, you just cry, you need to cry about this. You cry all you want, but what is your financial situation and what do we need to do about it?'

"The experience helped both of us to get more comfortable with money. She got through her fear of money, which had started in her family of origin and was reinforced in her marriage, where my dad controlled the money and she felt powerless. Finally, by going to work she was able to gain power and became able to talk about money and get through the grief. She doesn't cry about it anymore. She takes great pride in the fact that she is now supporting herself.

"I still feel nervous about money at times. When I first started saving my own money, separate from my husband's, I would break out in a sweat just going to the bank. You know, if I was moving $3,000 into an investment or taking it out to spend, I would just be in a sweat. I'd get scared that I might be doing the wrong thing and feared losing the money.

"Probably the best thing that I have done is start to read about money and learn about it. There is still a lot of secrecy about money. Women don't talk openly about it, especially specific amounts. I was at dinner with some female friends the other night and somebody said, 'Well, how big would this pension be?' I assumed they meant dollars, and I told them, and then my face got red and I said, 'You know I don't talk amounts.' But maybe we need to be able to talk more openly so that we can learn from each other. Men talk about these things and they find investment opportunities that way. It's a network kind of thing. I think that women sometimes talk about how they feel about money but not necessarily what we should do about it."

In terms of money, Cecily has come a long way from where she and her mother started. Although she's struggled, she has mustered the courage to develop increasing levels of financial self-sufficiency within her marriage. Since she started saving her own money separately from her husband's money, she has amassed independent investments of close to $200,000. She explains how this has happened. "When Bill and I got married I went to work as a nurse. I really didn't have a sense of long-term financial planning, but I remember putting money into my pension. Women were never encouraged to do that back then; people just assumed women wouldn't need pensions.

"As time went on, I had the children and stayed home with them. When they were both in school I went back to work. After I had the children I began to become more aware of the need for security down the line. I think the children mainly drove that, and also the realization that I still had to be able to support myself. I mean things happen in marriages and you never know how it will end up.

"Plus, I developed a friendship with an older woman who taught me some things about money. She had always had her own money separate from her husband. They had some joint money and they had separate bank accounts. Well, I had never heard of that – that a woman would have separate money!

"So I opened my own bank account and put some of my salary into it. I thought, 'Oh, Bill will divorce me over this, but I'll do it anyway!' As it turned out, it was never an issue. I just did it. I think my fear about doing it was a throwback to childhood. My father would have been upset with my mother if she had done that. That modelling was so influential. Anyway, that was the beginning of my success, having my own bank account.

"Having my own money gave me a sense of strength, a sense of choice. I could see that I was building something and that it is not a joint thing; it is mine and I was building my future security. That was really important to me.

"Bill has some of his own savings, and we also have a joint account that he supports because, being an engineer, he probably earns three times as much as I did. He also feels responsible for supporting the family. So we take our living expenses out of the joint account and buy our discretionary items from our own money. I bought a computer, and if I take little trips I use my money. But if I needed money I'd just ask; it isn't a problem.

"I think that money isn't a problem between us because we have our own separate power with money. I think our marriage does better because of it. We are the kind of people for whom equality is a good thing, and financial equality goes hand in hand with that. There isn't any kind of power imbalance; it's more of a friendship with us. I don't have feelings of resentment because I don't have enough money and he doesn't have feelings of resentment over paying for everything or from supporting things that he doesn't believe we need.

"Things have really evolved for me. Last Saturday night I met with a group of women friends and we decided to start an investment club!"

It's great to hear about women like Cecily – women who have challenged themselves to take measures to ensure their own financial well-being. More and more women are doing this and, in the process, are gaining self-confidence, security and stronger relationships.

YOU OWE IT TO YOURSELF AND TO THOSE YOU LOVE

Unfortunately, not enough women adequately safeguard their finances within relationships. Half of all marriages today result in divorce, and, in the first year of divorce, the average woman's after-tax household income declines by 55 percent, whereas a divorced man's income declines by only 28 percent.[1] It's usually the woman who raises any children involved, and single-mother households account for 40 percent of the poorest 10 percent of our population.[2] So if you have kids, then you owe it to them, if not yourself, to take financial precautions. Manage your joint finances together in joint accounts.

Ignoring the possibility of divorce, you still face the possibility of outliving your spouse. Forty-seven percent of Canadian women over 65 are widows, as are 64 percent of the women over 75.[3] In Canada, women, on average, live seven years longer than men, and one-third of women retire at or below the poverty level. We all have a high likelihood of being on our own at some point during our lives, and the time to prepare for it is now. Isn't it better to take precautions early on and hope they are never needed rather then face the financial consequences later?

Toronto banking executive Nadine comments: "When I speak to women, I am amazed by how uninformed many of them are with regard to their finances. For example, I had dinner with some female friends, all of whom are university educated. We started talking about RRSPs and what they were invested in. They didn't know. We talked about life insurance. They didn't know what they had. Was their mortgage insured? They didn't know. Their husbands took care of all of that. What happens if their husband has a heart attack tomorrow? You need to know!

"For the financial health of your family you have to know your total financial situation. You have to document your assets, you have to have a will and an estate plan for your children to ensure that your wishes are carried out. I mean the worst time to deal with these matters is when you are in the middle of a family tragedy. That's also when people will take advantage of you. So you should always know what's going on with your family's finances. You don't want to compound a family tragedy – whether it's death or divorce – with a financial tragedy."

Nadine hit the nail on the head. Staying informed about your financial situation isn't just a good idea, it's a necessity. You owe it to yourself and to the people you care about.

It's a Matter of Respect – Self-Respect

So many women feel guilty about protecting themselves financially. One of the toughest positions to occupy and still maintain a belief in your financial worthiness is that of stay-at-home mom. Does not earning an income mean that you are less entitled to influence how your family's finances are managed? Many women struggle with that question. Some feel so guilty about spending "their husband's money" that even minor discretionary purchases, like buying themselves a new outfit, are difficult. When they talk about their family's financial situation, their comments are peppered with such phrases as, "he has the money," and, "I don't have any money of my own." Consciously or subconsciously, many women perceive their household income to be their husband's money and not theirs.

But is this really fair? If you and your partner switched places, wouldn't you want him to be protected? Wouldn't you value his contribution to the relationship equally with your own? Wouldn't you want your affairs to be in order so that if you died, he'd be informed enough not to be taken advantage of? Wouldn't you want him to be provided for in old age? Well then, treat yourself with the same level of respect.

Guilt Has No Place Here

It can be difficult to broach these subjects with a partner, particularly if you've operated in an alternative pattern for some time. But, if you feel guilty over your desire to be an equal financial partner within your marriage, then I suggest you change your view. First of all, quit comparing apples to oranges. For instance, if you are currently a stay-at-home mom, then your job is challenging and important. Your husband's job is equally important, but both jobs bear different fruit and are not directly comparable.

Assume your contributions are of equal value and that you and your husband should have equal access to the fruits of each other's labour. Just as you should not hoard your children's achievements and affection all to yourself, your husband should not hoard the fruits of his labour; namely, money.

Why Not Talk about It?

Lucy has been married for 15 years. Although she has a business degree, she has not worked outside of the home during her marriage, preferring to be home while her children grow up. As she describes it, the decision to stay home over the long term was not really a conscious one. Her husband earns an ample salary, taking care of her three children has kept her busy and she just never felt compelled to return to work.

Lucy feels lucky when compared to other stay-at-home mom's and, in many ways, she is. Although she still refers to it as "her husband's money," Lucy has equal access to the family finances and knows that she can talk her husband into any major purchase she really wants. Because she and her husband share very similar attitudes towards what money should and should not be spent on, deciding how to save and spend it is not a source of conflict for them.

Not everyone is lucky enough to marry a partner who shares her healthy financial attitudes. Carol, a middle-aged, not-for-profit administrator, and her husband, Jim, came from very different financial backgrounds. Carol explains: "I came from a well-off family. I had credit cards of my own and my university education was fully funded by my parents. My husband grew up with less money and was far less extravagant than I. When I married him, at age 20, I just sort of transferred all of the financial responsibility from my parents to my husband. It was very traditional, but I was happy to let someone else worry about the money. I'm sort of embarrassed about it now, and realize that I should have been involved.

"If I had it to do over again, I would work harder and sooner at getting to know how my husband makes decisions and would have been more involved in our finances. In the last 10 years, Jim and I have taken some courses that have helped us understand each other's personalities better and how we both gather information and make decisions. We've applied some of what we've learned to our money management, and it's a good thing too. Not only do I feel like I am sharing responsibility for an important factor in our family's future well-being, we are both paying more attention to our financial affairs. This is important because, although I hadn't realized it before, my husband was not spending as much time or attention on our family finances as would have been really optimal when he was the only one responsible for it. Now we are both responsible, we are both involved and the way we manage our money reflects a happy medium between my risk-taking attitude and his more conservative style. Our finances are probably in better shape and more organized now than they have been in years."

Carol and Jim have become more disciplined in how they manage their money, reviewing and discussing their finances on a monthly basis. Moreover, they've hired a financial planner to help them organize their investments and plan for the future. Their new arrangements have worked well for them.

I applaud Carol for taking the initiative to get involved, despite her initial fear that this might "rock the boat." Carol and Jim's mutual money management system is not the only good arrangement available, but it gives both of them more peace of mind and an increased sense of partnership.

Have you and your partner discussed the "nuts and bolts" of your financial management? Who makes most of the decisions about where money should be spent and invested? Do you know how much is invested and where? Do either of you have life insurance policies? Pension plans? Company shares? RRSPs? Do you have wills?

These are only a few of the questions that you need to consider in assuming personal financial responsibility and empowerment. It may seem daunting, but sometimes, as in Carol's case, the process turns out to be easier and more beneficial than you might expect, once you take the first step.

Making It Happen – Taking Care of Yourself in a Relationship

Here are some basic steps that you need to take if you are in a relationship:

1. Remain informed and actively involved in your family's financial decisions throughout your relationship.
2. If you and your partner decide that he or she will handle financial decisions for both of you, then you still need to remain fully informed. You need to understand the financial plan and how your assets are invested.
3. Make sure family assets are registered in both of your names. Your name should be on the mortgage as a co-owner. RRSP contributions should be made to your account regardless of whether you are working at a paying job. Even if you earn no income, money contributed to a spousal RRSP in your name can be used to reduce the contributor's taxes.
4. Develop a credit rating for yourself. At a minimum, make sure you have a credit card in your own name. Use it and pay the full amount owing each month. This will create a positive record of your consistent debt repayment.
5. Make sure that you have protection against catastrophic events. Each of you should have a will and each of you should know where your wills are kept. Whether you depend on one partner's income or need both partners' incomes to survive, make sure you have appropriate levels of life insurance. Make sure the surviving partner is the beneficiary in any pension plans or death benefits either of you have and buy income replacement disability insurance. (More on how to do all of this in Chapter 19.)
6. Make retirement plans, taking into account the fact that a female's life expectancy is approximately 80 years, while a male's is 72 years.
7. Should your marriage end, be sure to consider all of your family assets when determining the division of assets. If your spouse has a workplace pension, then you may be entitled to a share of it. CPP and QPP credits can be reallocated from him or her to you, and even frequent-flier points have been considered in some cases.

If you are single:

1. Plan for financial self-sufficiency. If you find someone who is able to meet your every need, then great, you'll have more than enough. If you don't, then you'll still be fine.
2. Get independent financial advice before you marry. If you bring considerable assets to the marriage, then consider a prenuptial marriage contract. If you

remarry and have children from a previous union, then think carefully about how you want to structure the distribution of your assets should you die. For instance, you can establish trusts that provide for a spouse during his or her lifetime and then designate where the remaining funds are to go after his or her death.

19

Covering Your Assets

Experience is a comb that nature gives us when we are bald.

CHINESE PROVERB

It would be a shame to work so hard for financial abundance and then lose it. This chapter briefly covers various ways to protect your money from unexpected events. The linchpins of doing this are wills and insurance.

WHERE THERE'S A WILL THERE'S A MUCH EASIER WAY

One in five Canadians has had a family dispute over inheritances, and one in four expect to experience conflict with family members over a will. Yet half of all Canadians and 44 percent of parents with children at home have not prepared a will.[1]

Regardless of your financial or personal state, you should have a will. Writing one can be very straightforward; all it requires is pen and paper. At a minimum, you should prepare a dated, signed document detailing how you would like your assets to be distributed upon your death. In some provinces your will doesn't even have to be witnessed by anyone else if it is in your own handwriting.[†] However, if you type your will or fill in one of the pre-printed forms that is readily available at office supply stores, then it will need to be signed by two witnesses who are neither beneficiaries nor your spouse. Personally, if you have

† This is not legally valid in British Columbia.

any significant assets or dependents, I would strongly suggest you use a lawyer to prepare your will. Involving a professional who is experienced in estates and trusts is a valuable safeguard towards ensuring that the particular details of your situation are adequately addressed.

If you die without a will, then there are bound to be problems. First of all, the process of distributing your assets is likely to be much slower, with provincial legislation (rather than you) determining what happens. It's also likely to be more expensive and conflict-ridden than it need be. Most important, if you have children, then they may be taken into public custody until their guardians are appointed. I'm sure this is the last thing that you would want to have happen.

When writing your will, it is wise to choose an executor. An executor is the person or institution you name in your will whose responsibility it is to carry out your last wishes and to settle your estate. An executor is typically responsible for arranging your funeral, filing your final income tax return, making sure your debts are paid and distributing your remaining assets as requested. Your executor may be a relative, a friend, your accountant, your lawyer or an institution such as a trust company. One sensible option is to appoint co-executors, one of whom is a family member or friend who knows your values and wishes and the other of whom is a professional with expertise in the execution of wills. Regardless of your choice, make sure your executor is willing to take on the job and knows where your will is kept.

Once you die, even if you have a will, your estate is not immediately settled. Listen to 34-year-old Kate's story: "I guess the first thing that became apparent when my father died was that he had a lot of stuff that had to be taken care of. Now that it is all over and I look back I think his financial planning was very good, but at the time, it didn't seem that organized. We had to look for a lot of different files and try to figure out what was what and where it was all located. It was a very long procedure and a lot to deal with when your only living parent has just died unexpectedly.

"There is a lot involved when someone dies. Financial institutions won't release the deceased person's assets until you go through probate, which is a legal procedure and the government's way of taxing what you have left behind."

Like most people, you probably haven't given much thought to what would happen if you died. Certainly few of us consider the financial details. But delayed access to your estate assets can actually be quite critical if you have dependants who need money to cover living expenses and pay for your funeral. The process of probate, which involves the provincial court reviewing your will and issuing an order confirming that it is valid, can be time-consuming.

Kate explains how her father ensured that she and her siblings had immediate access to cash when he died. "Luckily for us my dad had a life insurance policy that named us as direct beneficiaries. That gave us access to some the insurance money quickly and meant we didn't need to worry about paying for flights, funeral expenses and legal fees with our own money. It was a really good thing because my father died over two years ago and the estate is still not completely finalized. In part it's because he had a limited partnership that we haven't dissolved, but even without that it would still have taken a fair bit of time to wrap things up."

In addition to following Kate's father's tactic, you can hold financial assets and your home in "joint tenancy with right of survivorship." If you do this, then this property will immediately be shifted to the surviving partner without going through probate and, if the beneficiary is your spouse, without being taxed. Furthermore, you can name a beneficiary for any RRSP, RRIF and pensions you own. In most provinces, this ensures that the money in these plans goes directly to the beneficiary without going through probate.

If you plan to divide your estate between individuals or name someone other than your spouse as the beneficiary of your insurance policy or RRSP, then you should probably consult with an estate-planning professional to ensure that your actual objectives are met. For example, for the sake of simplicity, assume you have a husband and a 25-year-old son and you want to split your wealth between them. You have $100,000 in an RRSP and $100,000 in a GIC outside of your RRSP. You might assume that if you name you husband as beneficiary of the GIC and your son as beneficiary of the RRSP that they will each share equally in your estate. In fact, what would occur is that your son would be paid the $100,000 from the RRSP, but your estate would owe taxes on the RRSP proceeds. If you are in the 50 percent tax bracket, then your estate now owes $50,000 in tax. Your husband, therefore, would end up owing the $50,000 in tax and would only net $50,000 from his $100,000 GIC, minus the tax he would have to pay on your behalf.

As you can see, it is probably best for you to decide what your objectives are in terms of to whom you want to leave your wealth and how much you want to leave to each recipient. Then have a professional advise you on the most tax-effective and probate-efficient way to achieve your goals, given your circumstances.

Last, if the beneficiary is not your spouse, then you may wish to leave your assets to a testamentary trust with your chosen heirs as beneficiaries. They can also be named trustees in order to allow them to control the assets within the trust after your death. By doing this, your heirs can split income with the trust. In other words, when they take income from the trust they pay personal income tax on it. Any income that is generated by the trust, but left in the trust, is taxed at the same graduated personal tax rates as it would be if the trust were an individual. Hence, the lowest marginal tax rate applies to the first $29,500 of trust income.[2]

All of these steps can help ease anxiety and worry during trying times. Properly preparing for your eventual death isn't "dancing on your grave," it's showing that you care about others. Regardless of whether you devise complex professional estate plans or whether you write out your last wishes on a sheet of paper, it needs to be done. The sooner, the better.

While you are at it, you may also wish to assign enduring power of attorney to someone you trust. This will allow the assigned person to make decisions for you should you become incapacitated due to an accident or illness. The decisions you can choose to allow this trusted individual to make for you can extend beyond financial areas to medical care and even authority over where you reside and with whom you associate. For instance, this would give her the power to move you to a nursing home if she felt it was in your best interest. Again, this is a topic to discuss with your lawyer; however, the key is to assign "enduring" power of attorney rather than simply power of attorney because only enduring power of attorney remains valid should you become mentally incapacitated.

Ouch, That Hurt!

And now, on to a more pleasant topic – insurance! We'll start with a pop quiz! What type of insurance do you think is most important?

You might be surprised, but for many people disability insurance is most critical. Most people think life insurance is more important, but your chances of being disabled before you turn 65 are actually twice as high as are your chances of dying.[3]

Risk of Death vs. Disability[4]

Your Age	Probability of Death Before Age 65	Probability of Long-term Disability Before Age 65
30	23%	52%
35	22%	50%
40	21%	48%
45	19%	44%
50	17%	39%

Moreover, if you think the government will take care of you if you are disabled, think again. Even if you qualified for benefits under the stringent requirements, the maximum CPP benefit you could receive in 1999 was only $903.55 per month, plus $171.33 per child. So, if you would prefer a more comfortable lifestyle, then it makes sense to own disability insurance.

When purchasing disability insurance you will need to decide how long you would be willing to go without benefits before the insurance started paying out. Three months is typical, but the longer the time period you select, the lower your premiums will be. You also need to decide how long you would want the insurance to pay out. I recommend you select age 65 or life. You also need to decide how much you would want to be paid each month. If you are buying your insurance with after-tax dollars, then any benefits paid are tax-free. Ideally, many experts recommend a policy that pays 60 to 70 percent of your income. Additionally, you should ask for an "own-occupation" provision so that you will be paid if you can't work in your own occupation, not just if you can't work at all. Also, ask about residual benefits, which are paid if you can only work part-time.

Disability insurance is fairly expensive, so you may decide to compromise on some of the features you'd like. That's okay, just as long as you don't compromise on the concept altogether. If you earn an income, then you need disability insurance; and if you have an income-earning partner, then that person needs it too.

Money After Life

Luckily, life insurance is relatively inexpensive compared to disability insurance. That's a good thing, because unless you have no dependents or are near retirement age and have considerable assets saved up, you probably need life insurance. And if you are married but make a lot less than your spouse, then you should be the named beneficiary in a policy on his or her life.

The amount of life insurance you and your partner should have depends on a number of factors. The decision is up to you, but you should probably take into account funeral and estate settlement expenses, outstanding debts that would need to be repaid, the future cost of your children's education and the amount of income the surviving family members would need. You may also want to buy extra life insurance to cover the potential taxes that will need to be paid against your RRSP assets in the event that they aren't left to a surviving spouse. I'll let Kate explain why this is important.

"A lot of people don't know that if you leave an RRSP or tax-sheltered money to anyone other than a spouse, the investment has to be completely cashed and then the estate is taxed as if the deceased person earned all of that money in their final year. So if you have any sizable amount in an RRSP it is likely to be taxed in the top tax bracket. You can lose more than half of it to tax."

When buying your life insurance policy you can choose between various types. The two main types are term insurance and whole life insurance. Term insurance means you are buying an insurance policy for a temporary amount of time. As you renew the policy your premiums will rise, since the chance of your death rises as you age. Whole life is an insurance policy that lasts your entire life. This means that your premium rates are guaranteed for life but that you will be paying a lot more than you would for the equivalent term insurance in your younger years. Furthermore, there are policies that offer a retirement savings component in addition to insurance, and there are policies that pay benefits if you are diagnosed with a critical illness. As with stock market investments, you can make it as simple or as complex as you like. From my perspective, all that really matters is that you buy adequate protection for yourself and your dependents.

Stop, Thief!

Last, you should insure valuable possessions. This means having homeowner's or renter's insurance for your home and its contents. If you have high-value assets that are exempt from the basic content coverage, then you should insure them as well. In particular, expensive computer equipment, jewelry, art, antiques and furs are often not covered.

So if you have work to do in this area, get moving. Write your will and think about how much it will help your beneficiaries go on with living should you die suddenly. Then call a few insurance companies for quotes and put that missing insurance in place.

Making It Happen – Doing a Protection Inventory

Record the items on which you need to follow up.

Protection	In Place	Needs To Be Put In Place	Needs To Be Updated	Not Required
Wills - My own - My spouse's				
Disability Insurance - My own - My spouse's				
Life Insurance - My own - My spouse's				
Home and Contents				
Insurance				
Other Insurance				

20

The Jackpot

Patience, and diligence, like faith, remove mountains.

WILLIAM PENN

Wow, we've covered a lot of ground together! You've done well! You now have all of the knowledge you need to succeed financially. Money is your friend. Money wants to be attracted to you because money knows you have a plan. You have a mission, you have goals for your life and money wants to be your enabler. You just need to commit to your mission, believe in it and keep your eyes open for the opportunities that will appear.

You know the steps to take. You have the prosperity equation. Put it to work in your life.

Cultivate positive money attitudes	$
+ Waste less	$ $
+ Earn more	$ $ $
+ Invest wisely	$ $ $ $
+ Protect what you have	$ $ $ $ $
Achieve your financial goals	$ $ $ $ $ $
Achieve your life goals	♥♥♥♥♥♥♥

The more you work each element of the equation, the more potential you will have to realize the financial prosperity that will help you achieve your heart's desire – your deepest life goals. The money is there. As you eliminate the limiting beliefs that block you, you will see ways you never imagined before to increase your financial and personal prosperity. Cultivate positive messages in your mind. Set spending priorities. Respect money by not wasting it. Ask for what you deserve. Manage what you have. And protect what you accumulate. Work the prosperity equation and make the choice to harness the power of money in your life.

Remember that success requires both thought and action. Be clear about what you think and feel about money. Make sure your thoughts reflect your positive intent towards prosperity. Visualize success as you define it. Act to create opportunities for prosperity and actively surf for opportunity. Manage your money effectively on a daily basis. Thought and action work together; one without the other is not enough. You have the power and the strength to do both and to do them well. You have everything you need to succeed.

Nelson Mandela said, "Our deepest fear is not that we are inadequate, our deepest fear is that we are powerful beyond measure."[1] I believe this is true for all of us. Claiming our power as women and as citizens of this world is our responsibility, for it is through claiming this power that we can best contribute to our world. You have the power to succeed beyond your wildest dreams. Go for it.

The lesson is worthiness. You are worth it. You deserve it. Build your financial security, build your prosperity and claim your success in life. Through your thought and actions, mould your future. And as you do so, let other women witness what you've learned.

Notes

CHAPTER 1

1. Cindy Skrukwa, in-depth interviews with Canadian women.
2. Linda Silver Dranoff, *Women in Canadian Law* (Toronto: Fitzhenry and Whiteside, 1977), 10, 47, 48.
3. *The Globe and Mail*, 16 April 1998, A22.
4. Statistics Canada, 1996 Census (Ottawa: Minister of Industry, 1996).
5. Statistics Canada, 1981 and 1996 census data (Ottawa: Minister of Supply and Services, 1981/Minster of Industry, 1996).
6. *The Financial Post*, 28 January 1997, vol. 9, p. 3.
7. *The Edmonton Journal*, 3 August 1997, F3.

CHAPTER 5

1. Human Resources Development Canada website, www.hrdc-drhc.gc.ca/isp/
2. Malcolm Hamilton, William M. Mercer Ltd.

CHAPTER 8

1. Statistics Canada, Catalogue 13-217. (Ottawa: Minister of Industry, 1996).
2. Statistics Canada, 1996, Earnings Report, as reported in *The Globe and Mail*, 24 March 1998.
3. *The Globe and Mail*, 13 May 1998, A4.
4. Statistics Canada, 1996 Census. (Ottawa: Minister of Industry, 1996).
5. Ibid.
6. Ibid.

CHAPTER 9

1. Elizabeth Perle McKenna, *When Work Doesn't Work Anymore* (New York:

Delacorte, 1997), 51.

CHAPTER 10

1. Tara Parker-Pope, *The Wall Street Journal*, quoted in *The Globe and Mail,* 11 April 1998, B15.
2. *The Globe and Mail*, 26 May 1998, A3.

CHAPTER 11

1. Bank of Montreal, Economics Department, Statistics Canada data.
2. *The Globe and Mail*, 28 March 1998, D6.
3. Bank of Montreal, Economics Department, Statistics Canada data.
4. "Closing the Gap," *The Globe and Mail*, 28 March 1998, D6.
5. Dun and Bradstreet Information Services; and Bank of Montreal, Economic Department.

CHAPTER 13

1. Stock in unproven ventures, where the price per share is usually under $5.00 per share. It is only traded on the smallest stock exchanges or outside of stock exchanges altogether.
2. ScotiaMcLeod Inc., *Handbook of Canadian Debt Market Indices*. (Toronto: Griffin House Publishing, 1999).
3. *The Globe and Mail*, 4 February 1999, C9. (Sources: Datastream, ScotiaMcLeod, Frank Russell Canada, and Morgan Stanley Capital International.)
4. Comparison of the New York Stock Exchange – All Stocks Universe (including performance of all stocks on the NYSE, and starting in 1962, the AMEX and NASDAQ exchanges to other financial investments. Source: University of Chicago. (Royal Bank ad, November 1998)
5. Peter Lynch, *Key Things Every Investor Should Know* (Fidelity Management and Research Company brochure, 1998).
6. April Lindren, *The Edmonton Journal*, 30 August 1997, F2. (Source: Toronto Stock Exchange.)
7. Ibid.
8. Lynch, *Key Things*.
9. Kwok Ho and Chris Robinson, *Personal Financial Planning*, 2nd ed. (Toronto: Captus, 1996), 215.
10. Kay R. Shirley, *Live Long and Profit* (Chicago: Dearborn, 1997), 53.

CHAPTER 14

1. Peter Lynch, *Key Things Every Investor Should Know*.
2. April Lindren, *The Edmonton Journal*, 30 August 1997, F2.

3. Brad Barber and Terrance Odean, "Boys Will be Boys: Gender, Overconfidencce and Common Stock Investment" (unpublished working paper, University of California at Davis, 1999).
4. *The Globe and Mail*, 17 April 1999, B6.

CHAPTER 15

1. *The Globe and Mail*, 23 November 1999, B3.
2. *Maclean's Guide to Personal Finance* (Toronto: Maclean Hunter, 1999), 34.

CHAPTER 16

1. CIBC Personal Banker Phone Line, 1-800-465-2422.

CHAPTER 18

1. Ross Finnie, "The Economics of Divorce," in *Family Matters: New Policies For Divorce, Lone Mothers and Child Poverty* (Toronto: C. D. Howe Institute, 1995), 105.
2. Bruce Little, "Poverty is Single and She Has a Child," *The Globe and Mail*, 8 March 1999, A2.
3. Monica Townson, *Independent Means: A Canadian Woman's Guide to Pensions and a Secure Financial Future* (Toronto: Macmillan, 1997), 9-10. Statistics Canada data.

CHAPTER 19

1. Michael Kane, *The Calgary Herald*, 21 November 1998, A18.
2. "How to Make Your Assets Grow," *The Globe and Mail*, 25 April 1998, B22.
3. Vicki Barnett, *The Calgary Herald*, 18 November 1998, F5.
4. Ibid.

CHAPTER 20

1. Nelson Mandela, inaugural speech, 1994.

Bibliography

BOLLES, RICHARD NELSON. *What Color is Your Parachute?* Berkley, CA: Ten Speed Press. 1997.

CANADA MORTGAGE AND HOUSING CORPORATION. *The Complete Guide to Buying Your Home.* Canada: Canada Mortgage and Housing Corporation. 1997.

CIMORONI, SANDY, BETH GRUDZINSKI, AND PATRICIA LOVETT-REID. *Women in the Know: How to Build a Strategy to Achieve Financial Success.* Toronto: Key Porter. 1997.

FOOT, DAVID AND DANIEL STOFFMAN. *Boom, Bust and Echo.* Toronto: Macfarlane, Walter, Ross. 1998.

MAGGIO, ROSALIE, COMP. *The Beacon Book of Quotations By Women.* Boston: Beacon. 1992.

SHIRLEY, KAY R. *Live Long and Profit.* Chicago: Dearborn. 1997

STIBBS, ANN. *Like a Fish Needs a Bicycle.* London, U.K.: Bloomsbury. 1992.

Index